PIANO · VOCAL · GUITAR   2ND EDITION

THE BIG BOOK OF
BROADWAY

ISBN 0-7935-3154-3

HAL•LEONARD®
CORPORATION
7777 W. BLUEMOUND RD. P.O. BOX 13819 MILWAUKEE, WI 53213

Visit Hal Leonard Online at
www.halleonard.com

CONTENTS

ALL I ASK OF YOU
(From "THE PHANTOM OF THE OPERA")

Music by ANDREW LLOYD WEBBER
Lyrics by CHARLES HART
Additional Lyrics by RICHARD STILGOE

here, with you, be-side you, to guard you and to guide you.

Christine: All I ask is ev-ery wak-ing mo-ment, turn my head with talk of

sum-mer-time. Say you need me with you now and al-ways;

prom-ise me that all you say is true, that's all I ask of

ANOTHER HUNDRED PEOPLE
(From "COMPANY")

Music and Lyrics by
STEPHEN SONDHEIM

Allegretto (♩ = 112)

MARTA:

(dolce e leggiero)

An-oth-er hun-dred peo-ple just got off of the train And came up through the ground While an-oth-er hun-dred peo-ple just got off of the bus And are look-ing a round At an-

oth - er hun-dred peo - ple who got off of the plane And are look-ing at us Who got

off of the train And the plane and the bus May - be yes - ter - day.

It's a ci - ty of strang - ers,

Some come to work, some to play. A ci - ty of strang - ers,

dust - y trees with the bat-tered barks, _____ And they

walk to-geth - er past the post - ered walls with the crude re - marks. _____

And they

cresc.

meet at par - ties through the friends of friends who they hard-ly know. _____

mf

Will you pick me up ___ or do I meet you there ___ or shall we

let it go? _____ Did you get my mes - sage 'cause I

looked in vain? Can we see each oth - er Tues-day, if it does-n't rain? ___ Look, I'll

call you in the morn-ing or my ser-vice will ex - plain. _____

poco cresc.

(dim.)

oth - er hun-dred peo-ple just got off of the train _ And an - oth - er hun-dred peo-ple just got

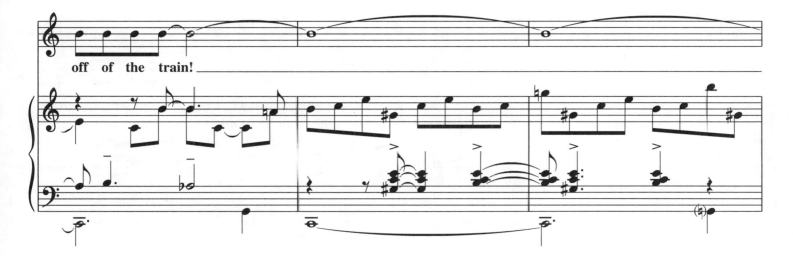

off of the train! _____

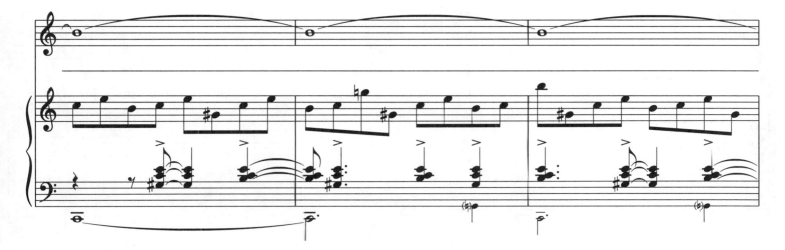

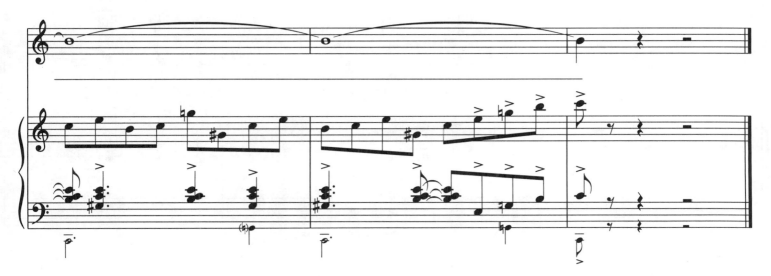

ANYTHING YOU CAN DO

(From The Stage Production "ANNIE GET YOUR GUN")

Words and Music by
IRVING BERLIN

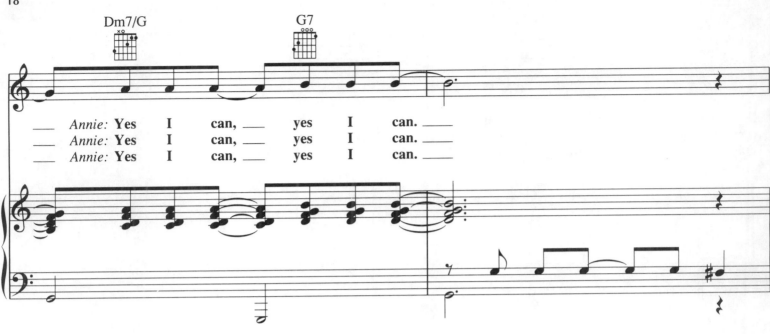

Annie: **Yes** I can, ___ yes I can. ___
Annie: **Yes** I can, ___ yes I can. ___
Annie: **Yes** I can, ___ yes I can. ___

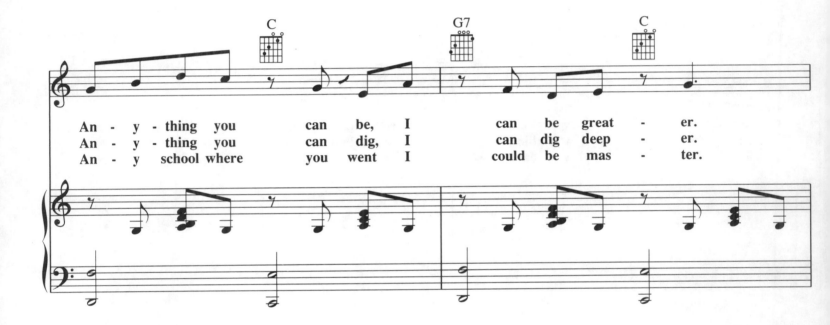

An - y - thing you can be, I can be great - er.
An - y - thing you can dig, I can dig deep - er.
An - y school where you went I could be mas - ter.

soon - er or lat - er, I'm great - er than you. ___ _Frank:_ **No you're** not. ___
I can dig an - y - thing deep - er than you. ___ _Frank:_ **Thir - ty** feet. ___
I could be mas - ter much fast - er than you. ___ _Frank:_ **Can you** spell.

Annie: **Yes I am.** _Frank:_ **No you're not.** _Annie:_ **Yes I am.** _Frank:_ **No you're not.**
Annie: **For - ty feet.** _Frank:_ **Fif - ty feet.** _Annie:_ **Six - ty feet.** _Frank:_ **No you can't.**
Annie: **No I can't.** _Frank:_ **Can you add.** _Annie:_ **No I can't.** _Frank:_ **Can you teach.**

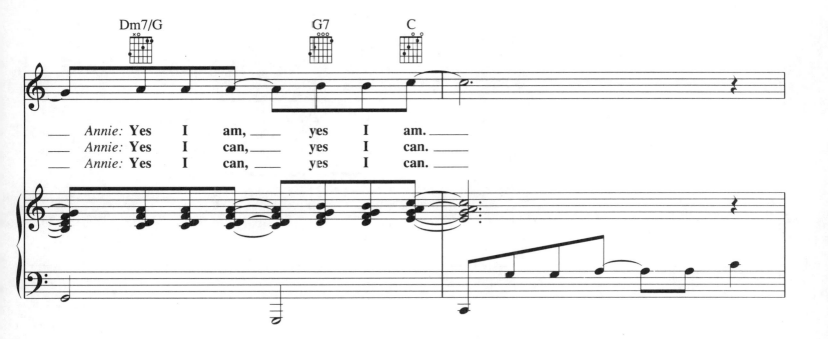

Annie: **Yes I am,** **yes I am.**
Annie: **Yes I can,** **yes I can.**
Annie: **Yes I can,** **yes I can.**

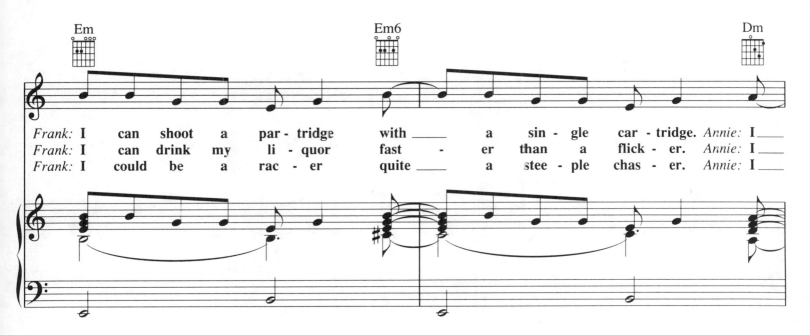

Frank: **I can shoot a par - tridge with a sin - gle car - tridge.** _Annie:_ **I**
Frank: **I can drink my li - quor fast - er than a flick - er.** _Annie:_ **I**
Frank: **I could be a rac - er quite a stee - ple chas - er.** _Annie:_ **I**

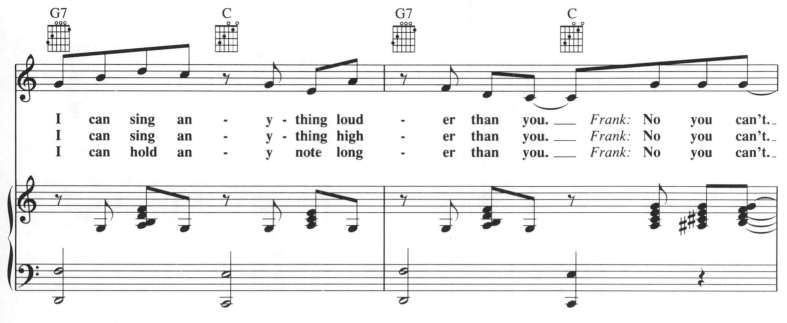

I can sing an - y - thing loud - er than you. ___ *Frank:* No you can't. ___
I can sing an - y - thing high - er than you. ___ *Frank:* No you can't. ___
I can hold an - y note long - er than you. ___ *Frank:* No you can't. ___

___ *Annie:* **Yes I can.** ___ *Frank:* No you can't. ___ *Annie:* **Yes I can.** ___ *Frank:* No you can't. ___
___ *Annie:* **Yes I can.** ___ *Frank:* No you can't. ___ *Annie:* **Yes I can.** ___ *Frank:* No you can't. ___
___ *Annie:* **Yes I can.** ___ *Frank:* No you can't. ___ *Annie:* **Yes I can.** ___ *Frank:* No you can't. ___

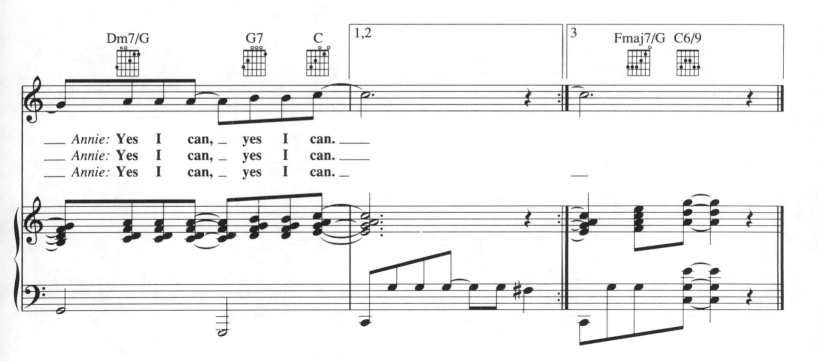

___ *Annie:* **Yes I can,** ___ **yes I can.** ___
___ *Annie:* **Yes I can,** ___ **yes I can.** ___
___ *Annie:* **Yes I can,** ___ **yes I can.** ___

BALI HA'I
(From "SOUTH PACIFIC")

Lyrics by OSCAR HAMMERSTEIN II
Music by RICHARD RODGERS

is - land! Come to me, come to me!" Your own spe - cial

hopes, Your own spe - cial dreams Bloom on the

hill - side And shine in the streams. If you try, You'll

find me, Where the sky Meets the sea. "Here am

BEAUTY AND THE BEAST

(From Walt Disney's "BEAUTY AND THE BEAST: THE BROADWAY MUSICAL")

Lyrics by HOWARD ASHMAN
Music by ALAN MENKEN

BEING ALIVE
(From "COMPANY")

Music and Lyrics by
STEPHEN SONDHEIM

* *Add notes in parentheses 2nd time only.*

33

not, Will want you to share A lit-tle a lot, Is be-ing a-

live, Be-ing a - live.

Some-one to crowd you with love,

Some-one to force you to care, Some-one to make you come

through, Who'll al-ways be there, As fright-ened as you Of be-ing a -

loco

8vb

live, ___ Be - ing a -

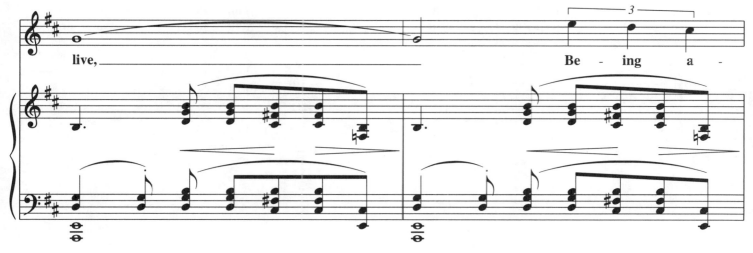

live, ___ Be - ing a -

live, ___ Be - ing a -

cresc. sempre

live. _____

_ff_

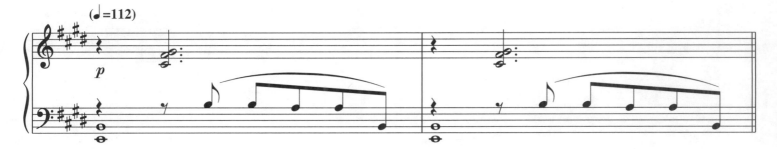

(♩=112)

_p_

Some-bod – y hold me too close,
Some-bod – y need me too much,

Some-bod – y hurt me too
Some-bod – y know me too

deep,
well;

Some-bod – y sit in my chair
Some-bod – y pull me up short

And ru - in my
And put me through

* _Add notes in parentheses 2nd time only._

38

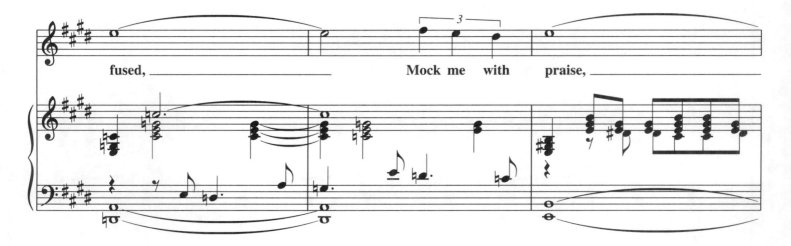

fused, _____ Mock me with praise, _____

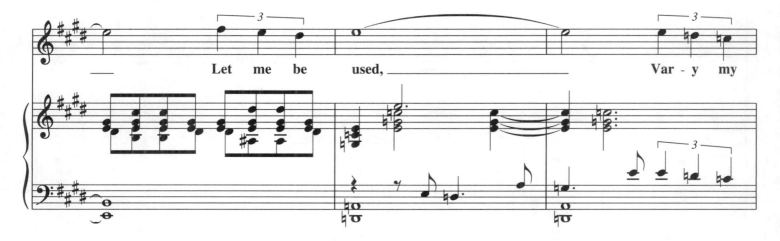

___ Let me be used, _____ Var - y my

days. _____ But a - lone _____

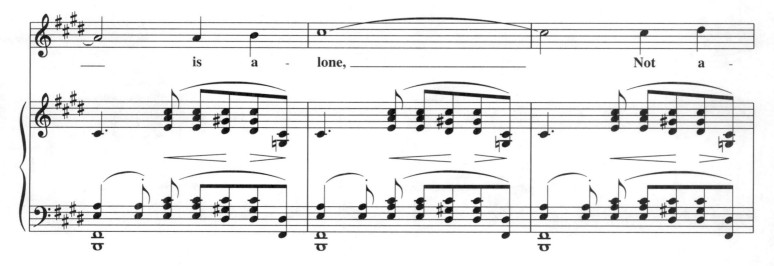

___ is a - lone, _____ Not a -

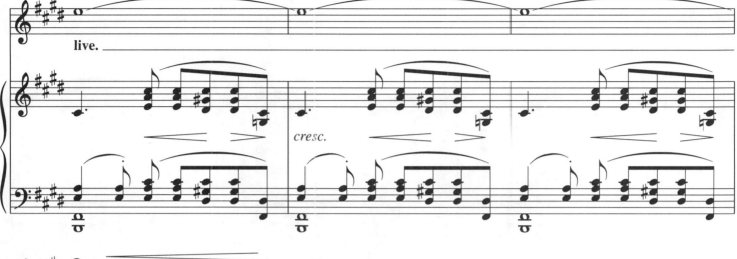

live. _____

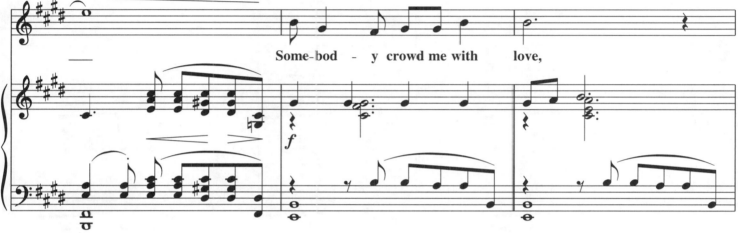

Some-bod - y crowd me with love,

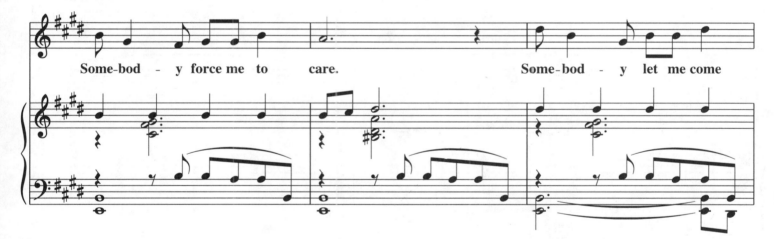

Some-bod - y force me to care. Some-bod - y let me come

through, I'll al-ways be there As fright-ened as you, To help us sur -

vive _____ Be - ing a - live, ____

___ Be - ing a - live, _____ Be - ing a -

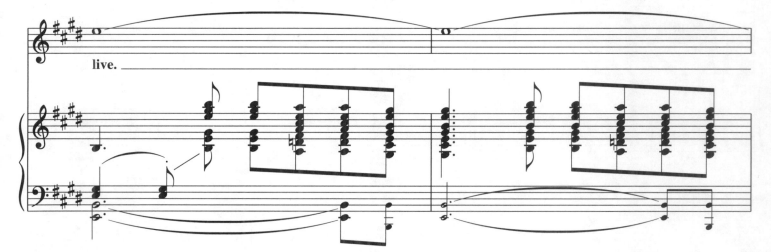

live. _____

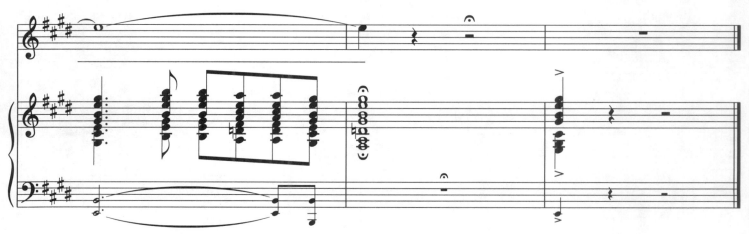

CLASS
(From "CHICAGO")

Words by FRED EBB
Music by JOHN KANDER

42

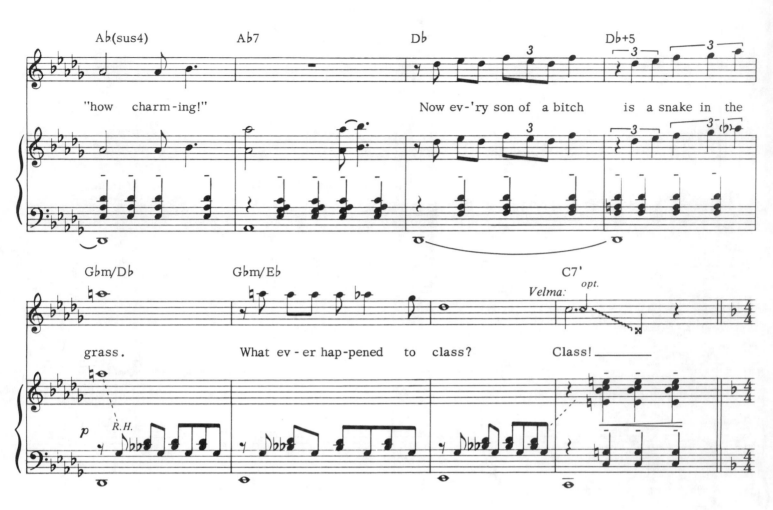

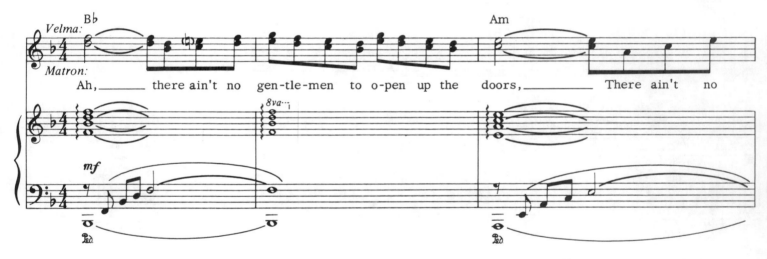

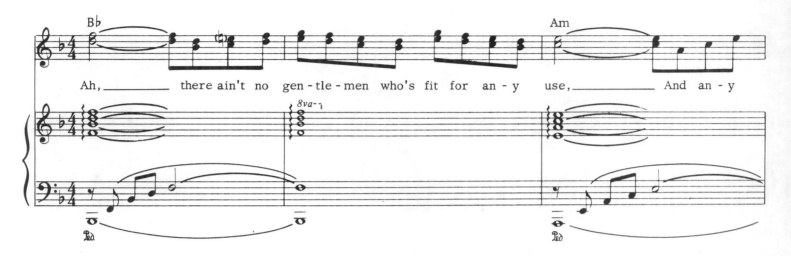

Ah, _____ there ain't no gen-tle-men who's fit for an-y use, _____ And an-y

girl-'d touch your pri-vates for a deuce.____ And e-ven kids-'ll kick your shins and give ya

kids-'ll kick your shins and give ya sass.

sass. No-bod-y's got no class.

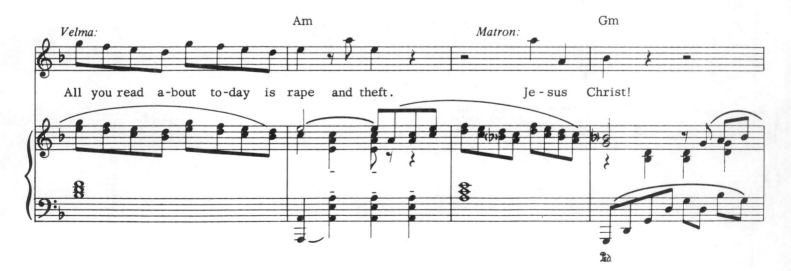

Velma:

Matron:

All you read a-bout to-day is rape and theft. Je-sus Christ!

BRING HIM HOME
(From "LES MISÉRABLES")

Music by CLAUDE-MICHEL SCHÖNBERG
Lyrics by HERBERT KRETZMER and ALAIN BOUBLIL

rest _____ hea - ven blessed. _____ Bring him

poco più mosso .... *rall.*

home, _____ bring him home, _____ bring him

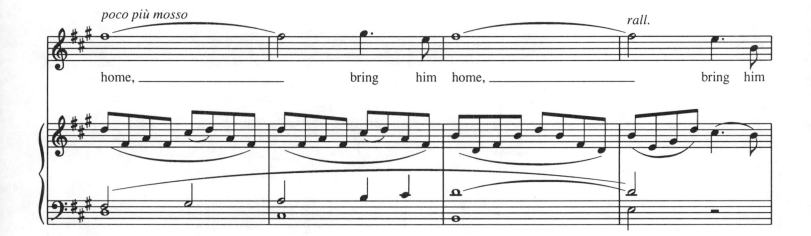

più mosso

home. He's like the son I might have known if God had grant-ed me a

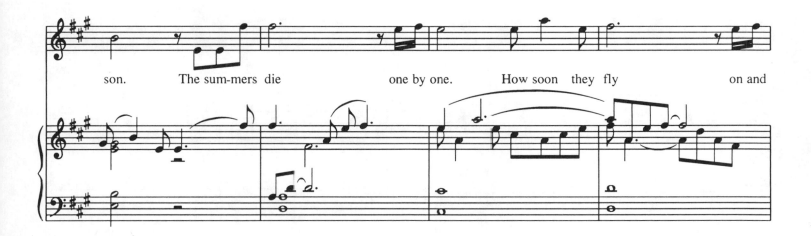

son. The sum-mers die one by one. How soon they fly on and

48

on.   And I am old   and will be gone.   Bring him

peace, _____ bring him joy. _____ He is

young, _____ he is on-ly a boy. _____ You can

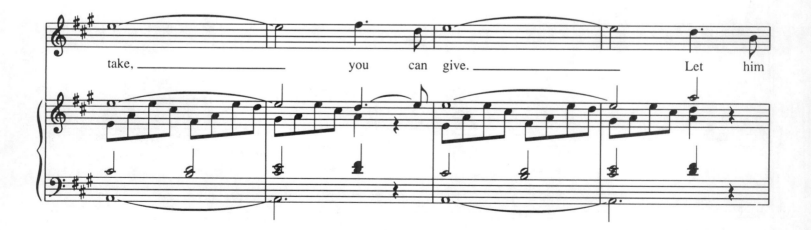

take, _____ you can give. _____ Let him

be, _____ let him live. _____ If I

die, _____ let me die, _____ let him

live. _____ Bring him home, _____ bring him

home, _____ bring him home. _____

BROTHERHOOD OF MAN
(From "HOW TO SUCCEED IN BUSINESS WITHOUT REALLY TRYING")

Handclapping Spiritual Feel

By FRANK LOESSER

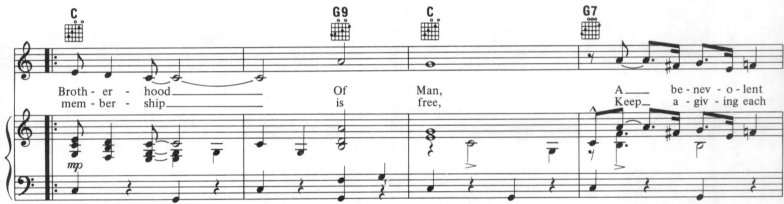

51

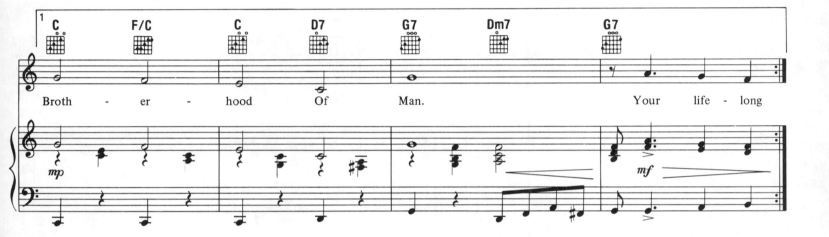

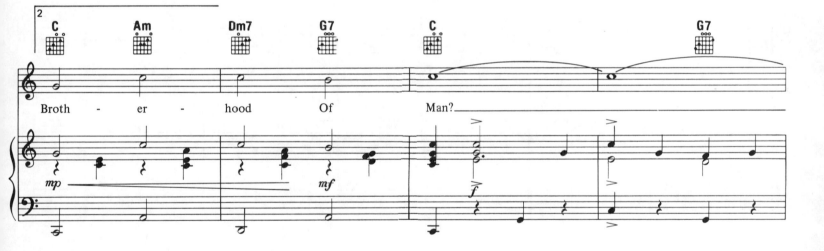

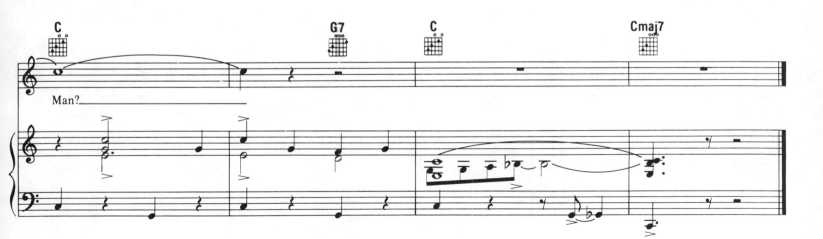

BRUSH UP YOUR SHAKESPEARE
(From "KISS ME, KATE")

Words and Music by
COLE PORTER

Bowery Waltz

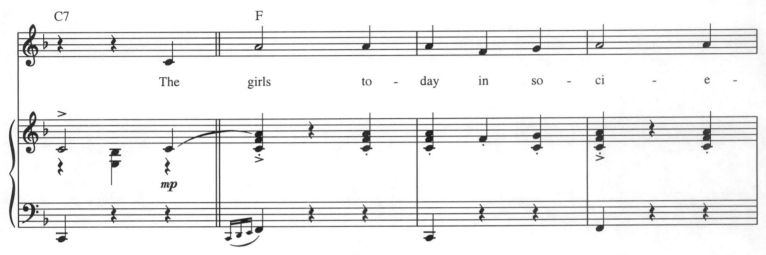

The girls to-day in so - ci - e -

ty Go for clas - si - cal po - et -

ry, So, to win their hearts, one must quote with

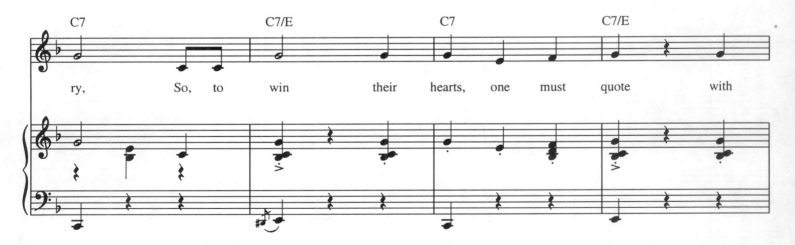

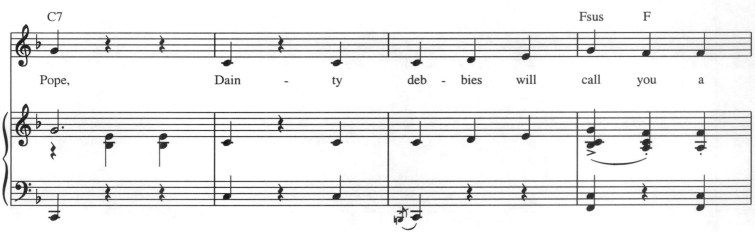

Pope, Dain - ty deb - bies will call you a

dope. But the po - et of them all _____

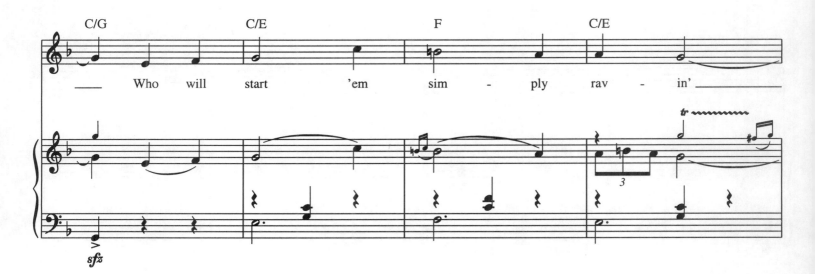

_____ Who will start 'em sim - ply rav - in' _____

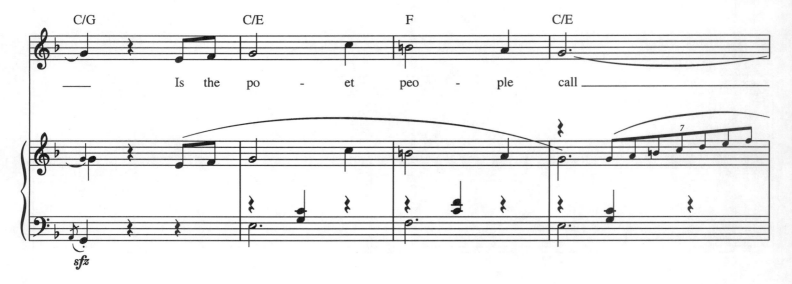

_____ Is the po - et peo - ple call _____

*Cockney for "take"

CAMELOT
(From "CAMELOT")

Words by ALAN JAY LERNER
Music by FREDERICK LOEWE

60

CLOSE EVERY DOOR
(From "JOSEPH AND THE AMAZING TECHNICOLOR® DREAMCOAT")

Music by ANDREW LLOYD WEBBER
Lyrics by TIM RICE

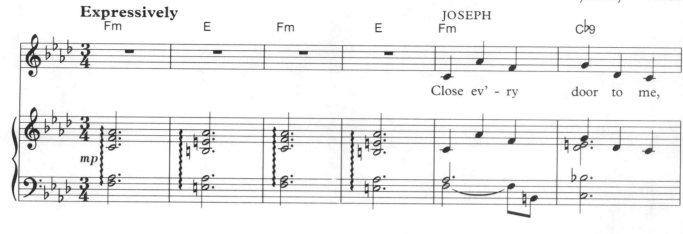

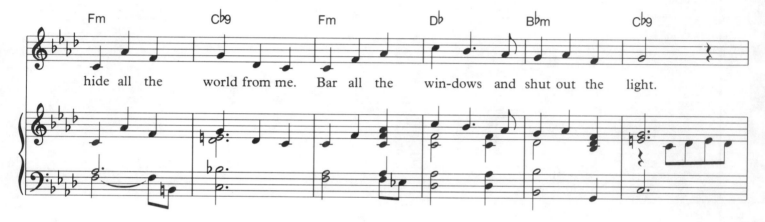

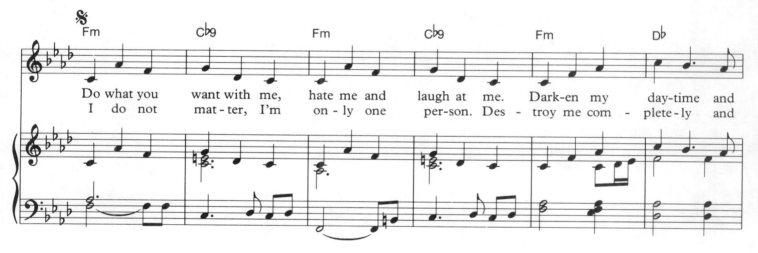

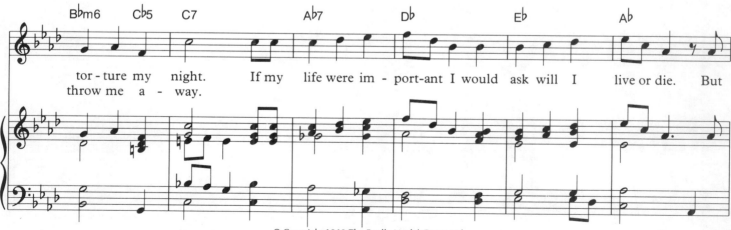

to Coda

I know the ans-wers lie far from this world. Close ev' - ry door to me, keep those I

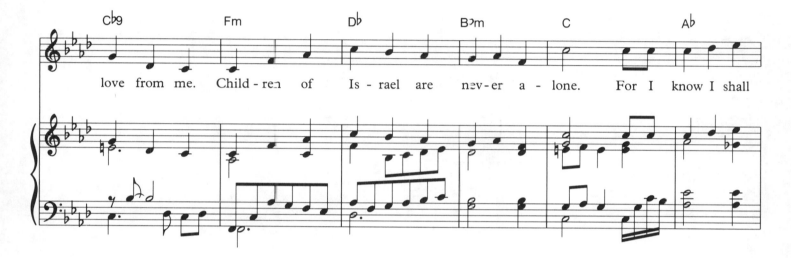

love from me. Child - ren of Is - rael are nev-er a - lone. For I know I shall

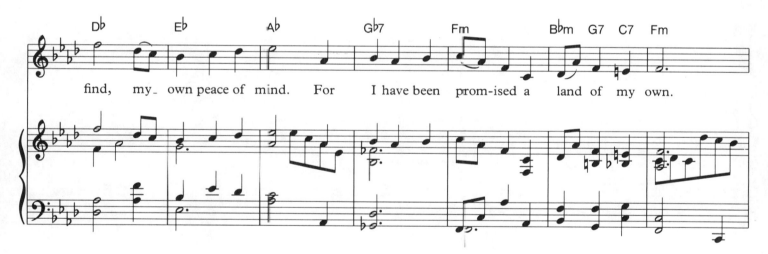

find, my own peace of mind. For I have been prom-ised a land of my own.

CHORUS

Close ev' - ry door to me, hide all the world from me. Bar all the

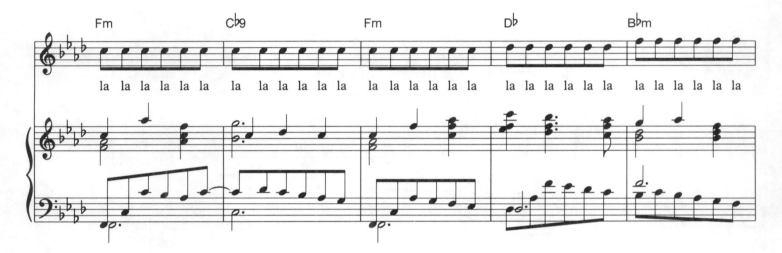

67

Da ℅ al Coda ⊕ e poi Coda

name. For - get all a - bout me and let me de - cay.

Close ev' - ry door to me, hide those I love from me. Child - ren of

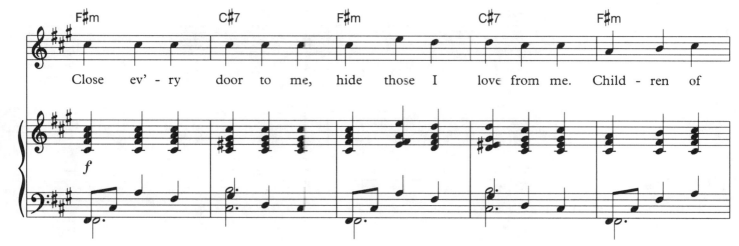

Is - rael are nev - er a - lone. For we know we shall find our_

own peace of mind. For we have been pro - mised a land_ of our own.

A COCK-EYED OPTIMIST
(From "SOUTH PACIFIC")

Lyrics by OSCAR HAMMERSTEIN II
Music by RICHARD RODGERS

When the sky is a bright ca-nar-y yel - low —

— I for - get ev-'ry cloud I've ev - er seen, — So they

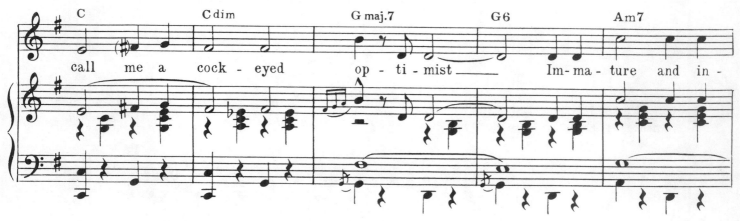

call me a cock - eyed op - ti - mist — Im-ma - ture and in -

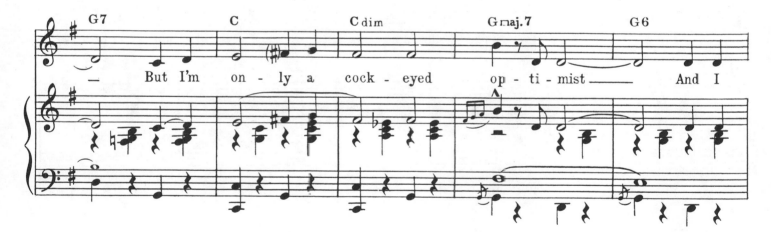

70

71

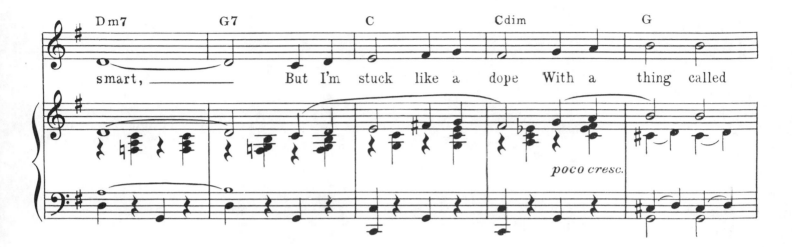

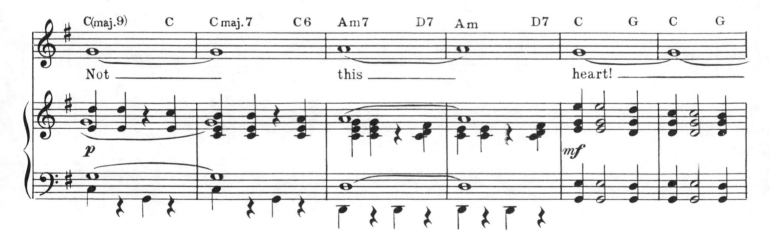

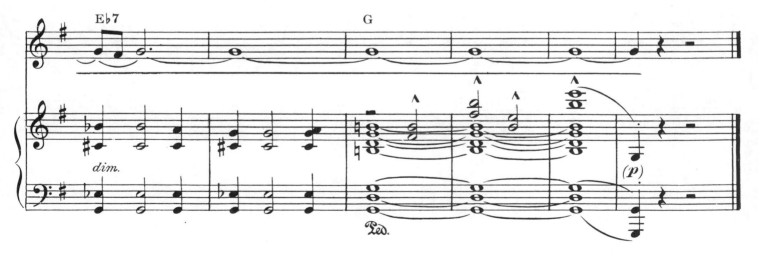

DANCE: TEN; LOOKS: THREE

(From "A CHORUS LINE")

Music by MARVIN HAMLISCH
Lyric by EDWARD KLEBAN

Dance:__ Ten;   Looks: Three__   is like to die.____
Fix.__ the   chas - sis, ____   "How do you do!"__

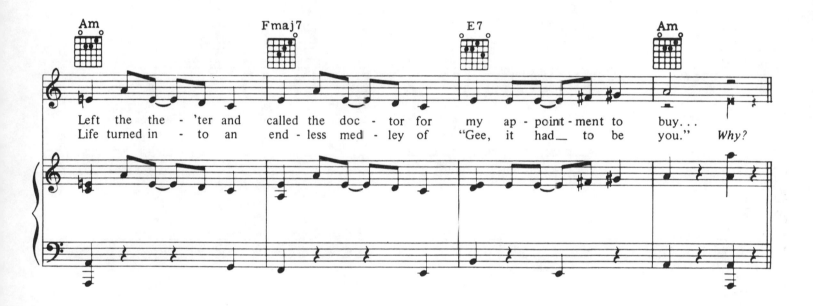

Left the the - 'ter and   called the doc - tor for   my ap - point - ment to   buy. . .
Life turned in - to an   end - less med - ley of   "Gee, it had__ to be   you."   *Why?*

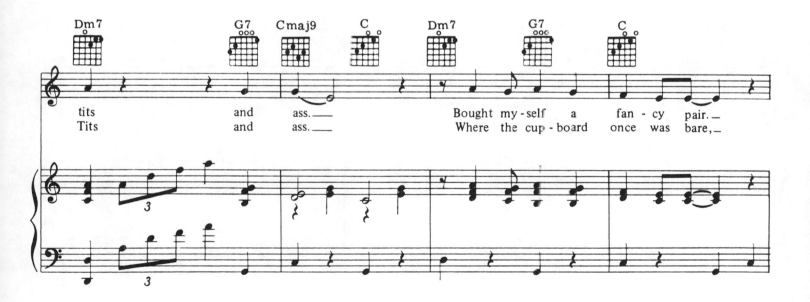

tits   and   ass.__   Bought my - self   a   fan - cy   pair.__
Tits   and   ass.__   Where the cup - board   once was   bare,__

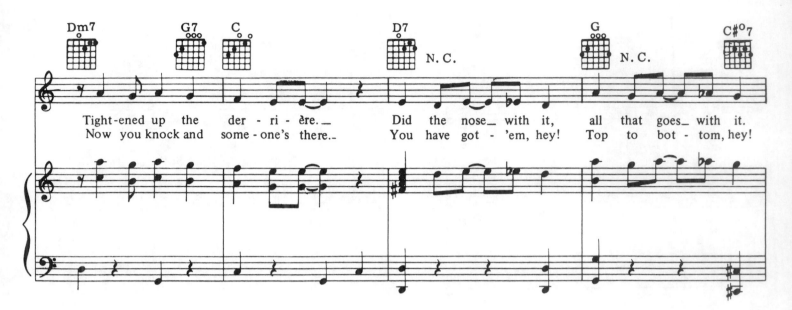

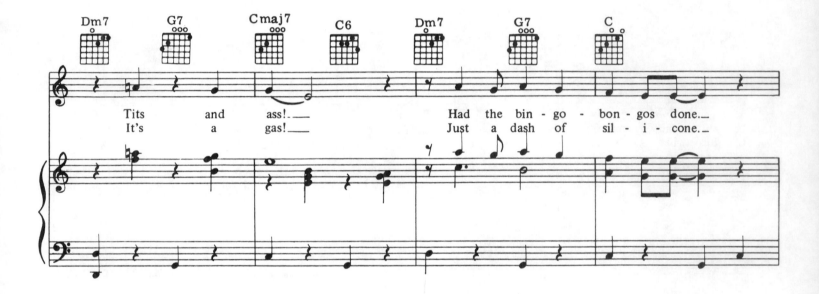

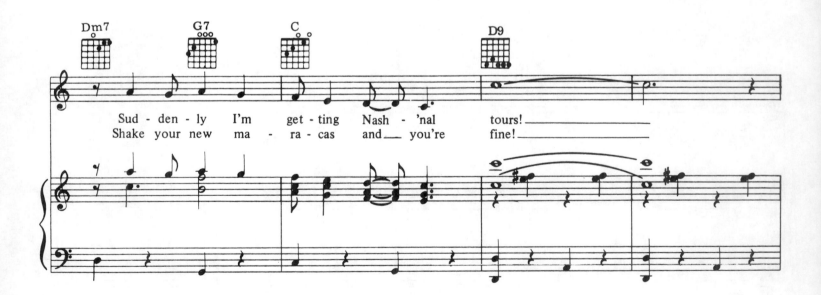

DON'T CRY FOR ME ARGENTINA
(From "EVITA")

Words by TIM RICE
Music by ANDREW LLOYD WEBBER

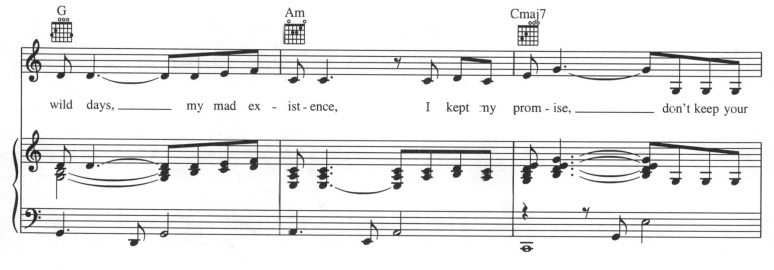

wild days, _____ my mad ex - ist - ence, I kept my prom - ise, _____ don't keep your

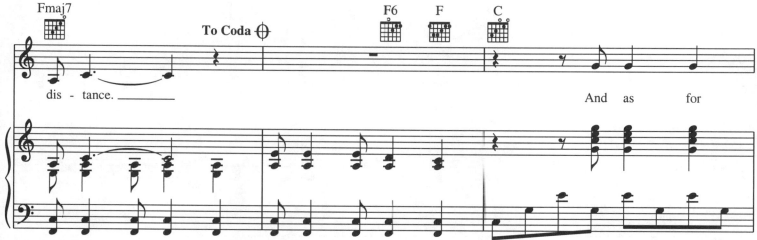

dis - tance. _____ And as for

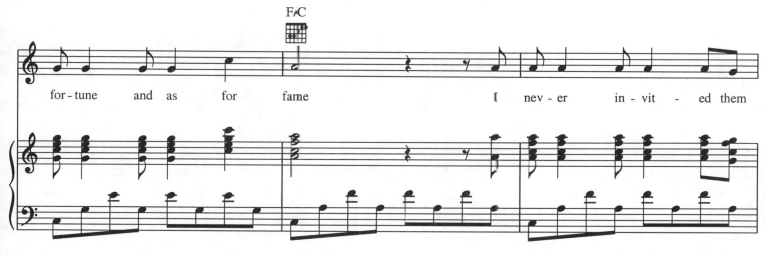

for - tune and as for fame I nev - er in - vit - ed them

in: Though it seemed to the world they were all I de - sired.

all you have to do is look at me to know that ev-'ry word is true.

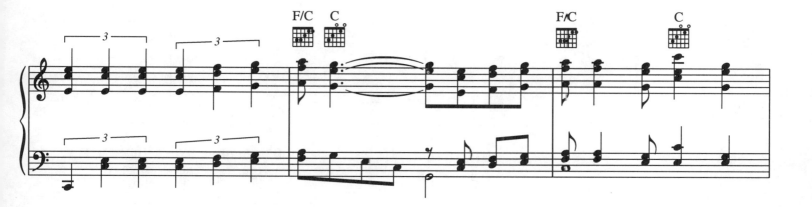

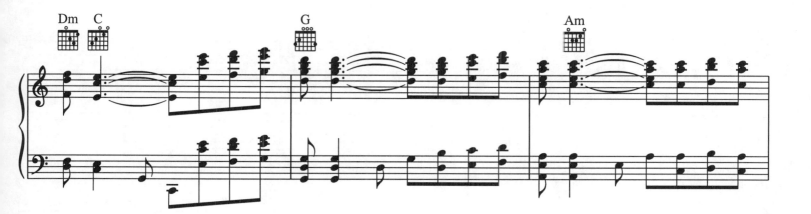

EVERYTHING'S COMING UP ROSES
(From "GYPSY")

Words by STEPHEN SONDHEIM
Music by JULE STYNE

I GOT THE SUN IN THE MORNING

(From The Stage Production "ANNIE GET YOUR GUN")

Words and Music by
IRVING BERLIN

Light bounce

Tak - ing stock __ of what I have __ and what I have - n't, _____ what do I find? __ The things I've got will keep me sat - is - fied. _____

92

93

THE GIRL THAT I MARRY

(From The Stage Production "ANNIE GET YOUR GUN")

Words and Music by
IRVING BERLIN

HELLO, DOLLY!

(From "HELLO, DOLLY!")

Music and Lyric by
JERRY HERMAN

HELLO, YOUNG LOVERS
(From "THE KING AND I")

Lyrics by OSCAR HAMMERSTEIN II
Music by RICHARD RODGERS

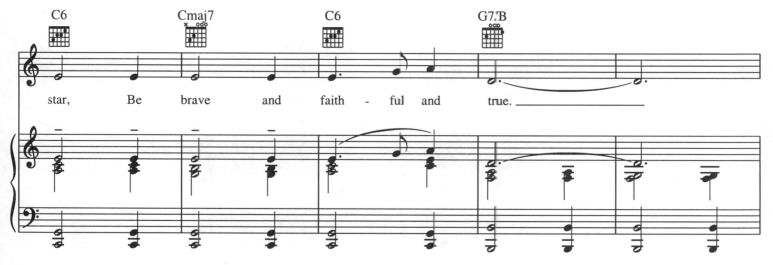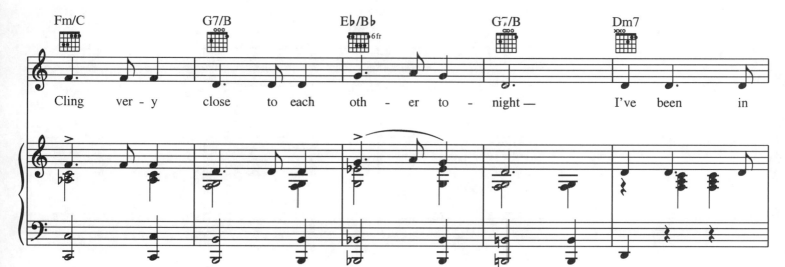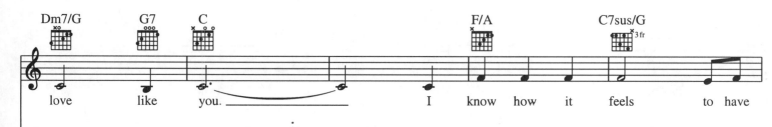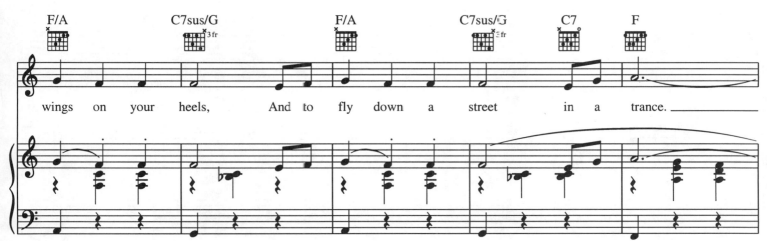

104

HONEY BUN
(From "SOUTH PACIFIC")

Lyrics by OSCAR HAMMERSTEIN II
Music by RICHARD RODGERS

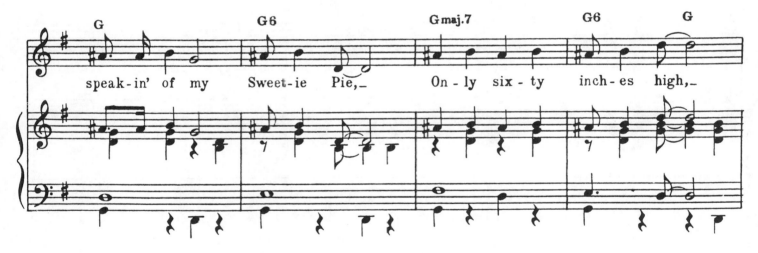

hair is blond and cur - ly, Her curls are hur - ly bur - ly. Her

lips are_ pips!_ I call her hips:_ "Twirl - y"_ and "Whirl - y."_

She's my ba - by, I'm her pap!_ I'm her boob - y, She's my trap!_

I am caught and I don't want-a run_ 'Cause I'm hav - in' so much fun with Hon - ey-

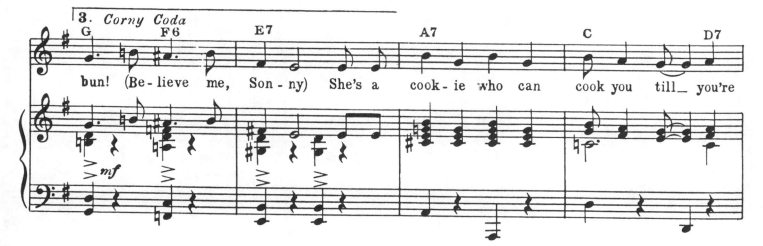

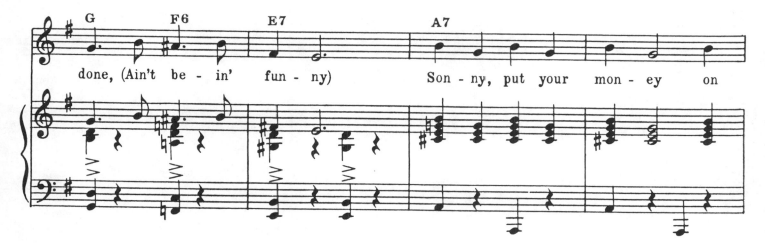

I AIN'T DOWN YET
(From "THE UNSINKABLE MOLLY BROWN")

By MEREDITH WILLSON

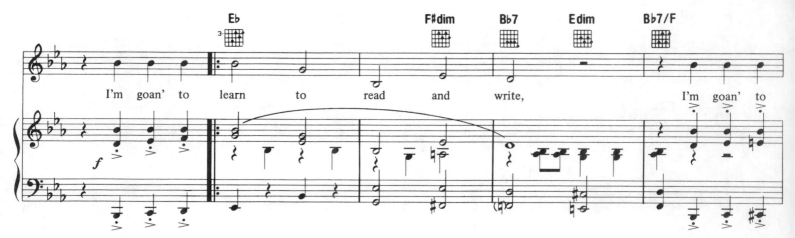

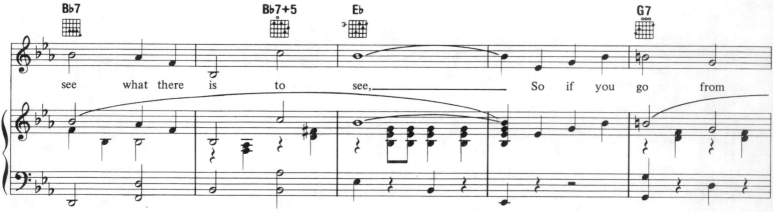

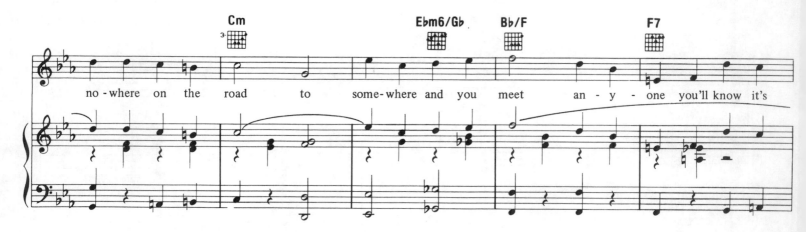

I DREAMED A DREAM
(From "LES MISÉRABLES")

Music by CLAUDE-MICHEL SCHÖNBERG
Lyrics by HERBERT KRETZMER
Original Text by ALAIN BOUBLIL and JEAN-MARC NATEL

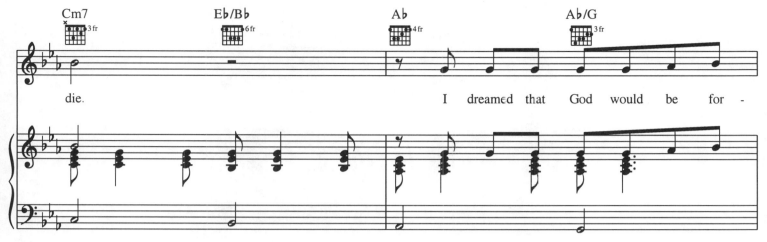

die. I dreamed that God would be for-

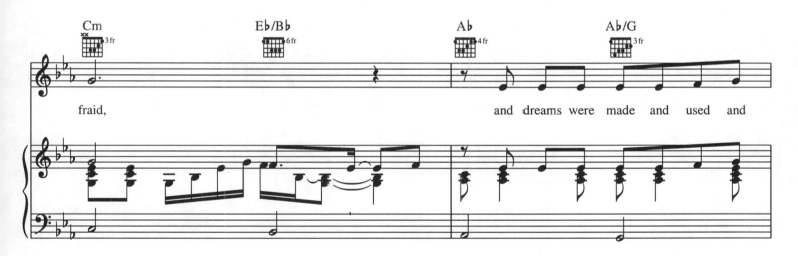

giv- ing. Then I was young and un-a-

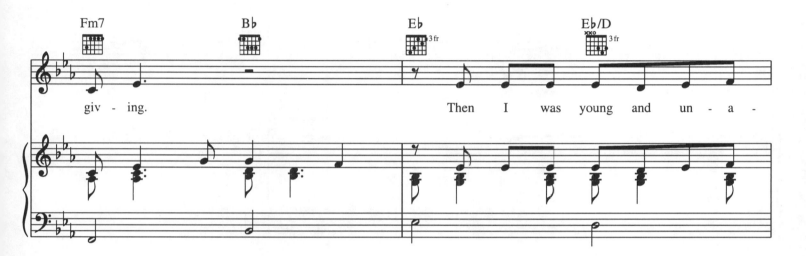

fraid, and dreams were made and used and

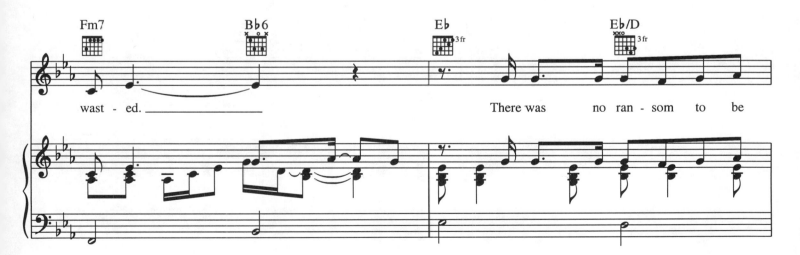

wast- ed. _____ There was no ran-som to be

paid,   so song un - sung, no wine un - tast - ed.

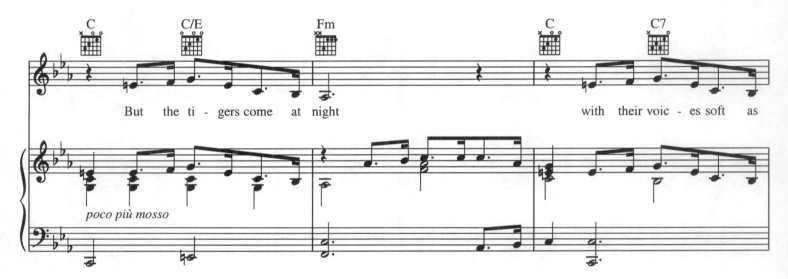

But the ti - gers come at night   with their voic - es soft as

poco più mosso

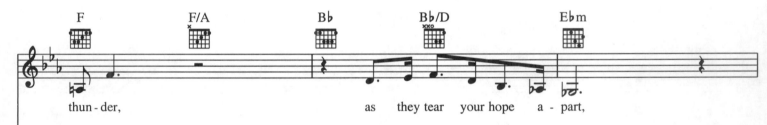

thun - der,   as they tear your hope a - part,

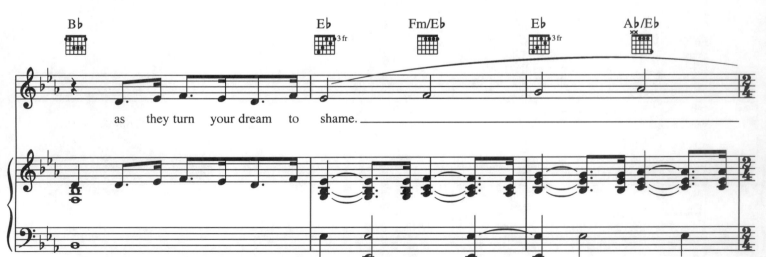

as they turn your dream to shame. _____

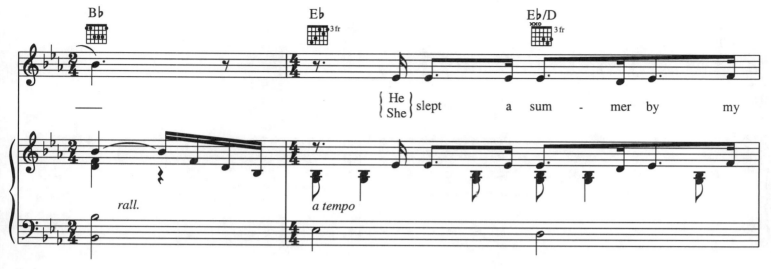

He/She slept a sum - mer by my

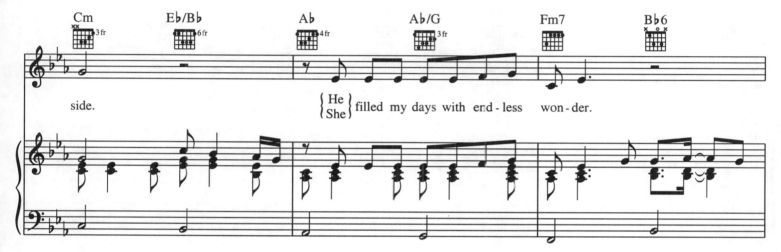

side. He/She filled my days with end-less won-der.

He/She took my child-hood in his/her stride, but he/she was gone when au-tumn

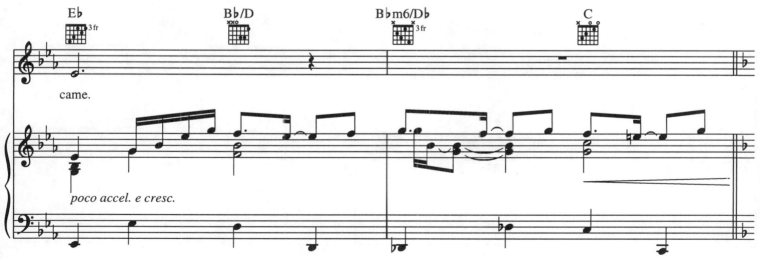

came.

poco accel. e cresc.

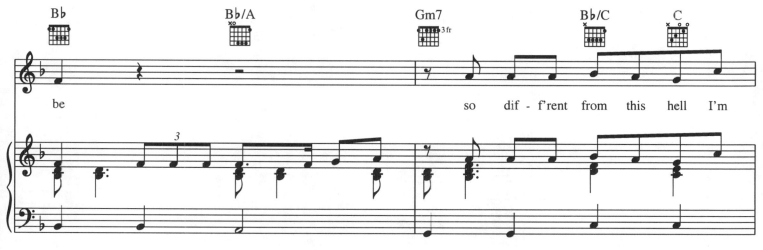

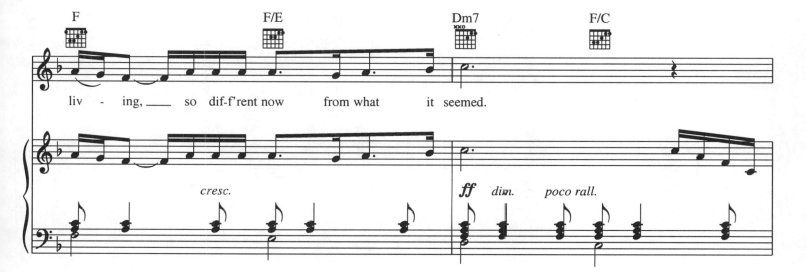

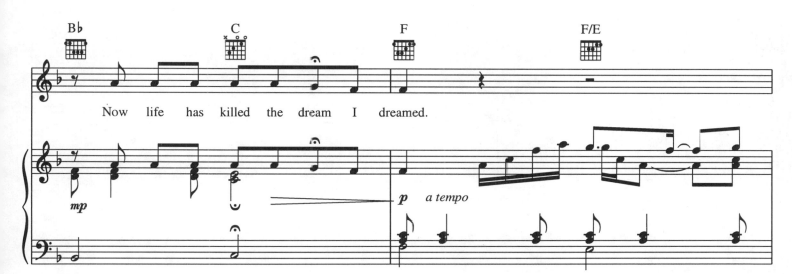

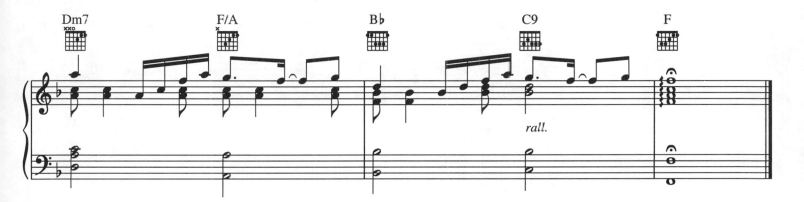

I'VE NEVER BEEN IN LOVE BEFORE
(From "GUYS AND DOLLS")

By FRANK LOESSER

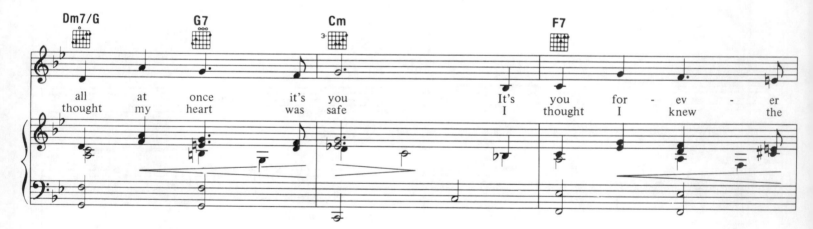

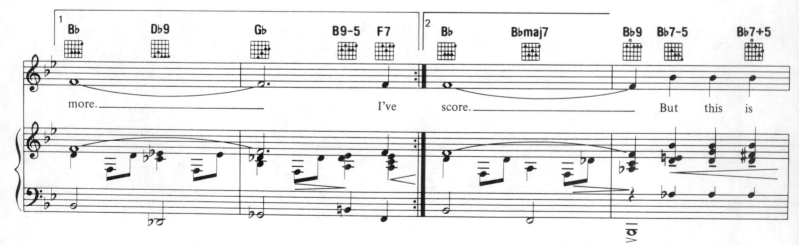

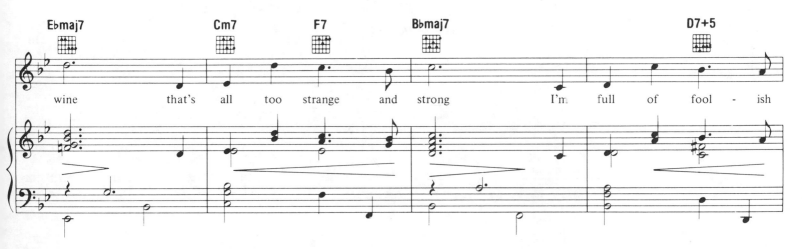

Ebmaj7 Cm7 F7 Bbmaj7 D7+5
wine that's all too strange and strong I'm full of fool - ish
Gm C7 A7 D A7 F7 F7-5
song and out my song must pour So please for -
Bb Gm Cm7 F7 F7+5 Bbmaj7 Dm7/G G7
give this help - less haze I'm in I've real - ly nev - er
Cm Cm7 F7-9 Bb Eb Gbdim Bb
been in love be - fore.

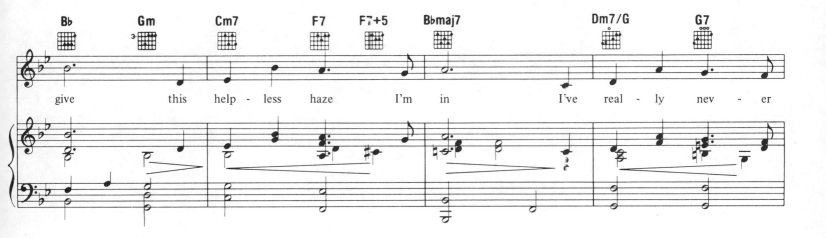

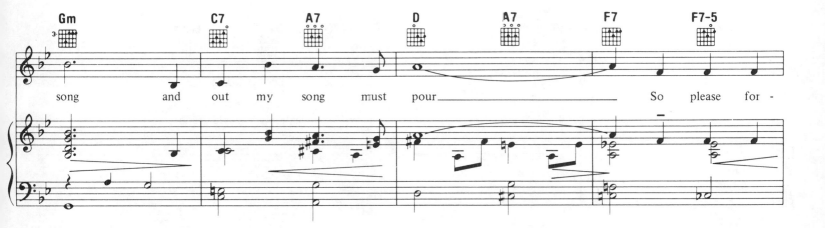

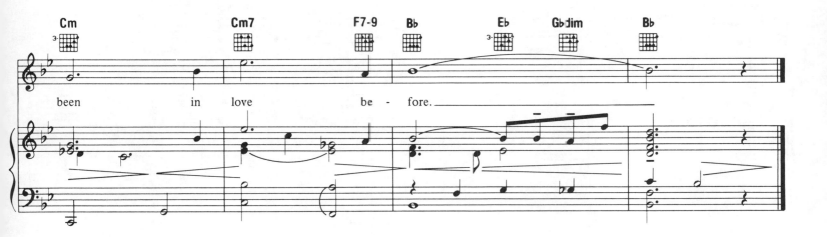

IF HE WALKED INTO MY LIFE

(From "MAME")

Music and Lyric by
JERRY HERMAN

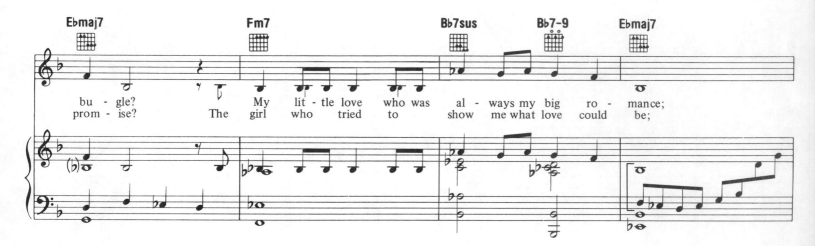

IF I CAN'T LOVE HER

(From Walt Disney's "BEAUTY AND THE BEAST: THE BROADWAY MUSICAL")

Music by ALAN MENKEN
Lyrics by TIM RICE

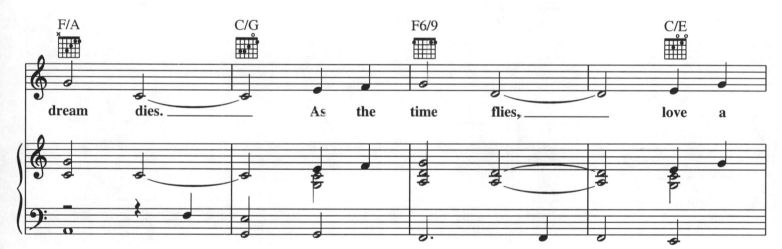

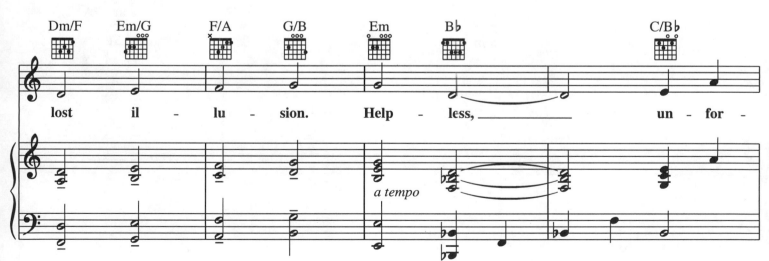

IF I LOVED YOU
(From "CAROUSEL")

Lyrics by OSCAR HAMMERSTEIN II
Music by RICHARD RODGERS

THE LAST NIGHT OF THE WORLD

(From "MISS SAIGON")

Music by CLAUDE-MICHEL SCHÖNBERG
Lyrics by RICHARD MALTBY JR. and ALAIN BOUBLIL
Adapted from original French Lyrics by ALAIN BOUBLIL

138

141

THE IMPOSSIBLE DREAM
(The Quest)
(From "MAN OF LA MANCHA")

Lyric by JOE DARION
Music by MITCH LEIGH

Tempo di Bolero

1. To dream _____ the im-pos-si-ble dream, _____ to
(2. To) right _____ the un-right-a-ble wrong, _____ to

fight _____ the un-beat-a-ble foe, _____ To
love _____ pure and chaste from a-far, _____ To

bear _____ with un-bear-a-ble sor-row, _____ to
try _____ when your arms are too wea-ry, _____ to

148

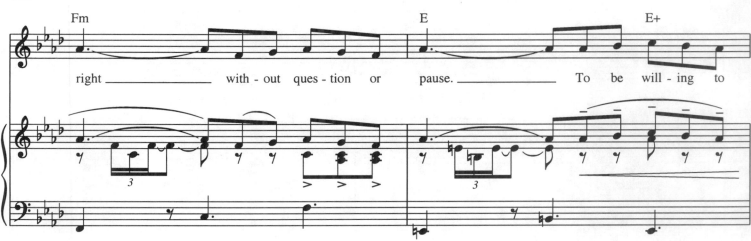

right _____ with-out ques-tion or pause. _____ To be will-ing to

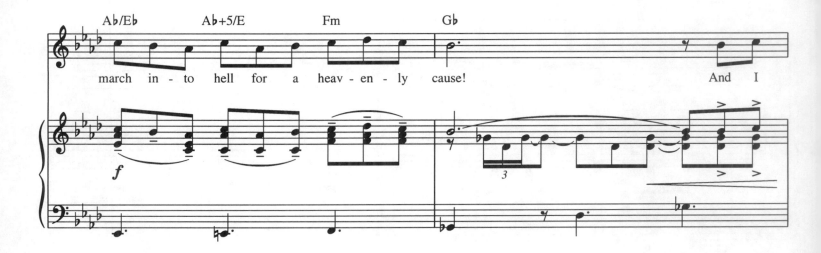

march in-to hell for a heav-en-ly cause! And I

know, _____ if I'll on-ly be true _____ To this glo-ri-ous

quest, _____ that my heart _____ will lie peace-ful and

calm, ____ When I'm laid to my rest, And the world ____ will be bet-ter for

this; ____ That one man, ____ scorned and cov-ered with

scars, ____ Still strove ____ with his last ounce of cour-age, ____ To

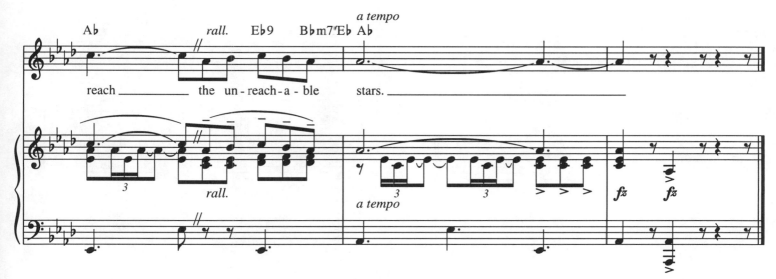

reach ____ the un-reach-a-ble stars. ____

THE JOINT IS JUMPIN'
(From "AIN'T MISBEHAVIN'")

Words by ANDY RAZAF and J.C. JOHNSON
Music by THOMAS "FATS" WALLER

Tempo di-sturb de neighbors

LEANING ON A LAMP POST

(From "ME AND MY GIRL")

By NOEL GAY

155

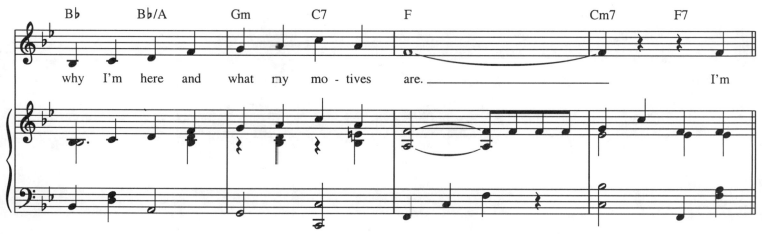

why I'm here and what my mo-tives are. _____ I'm

lean-ing on a lamp-post at the cor-ner of the street, In case a cer-tain lit-tle la-dy comes

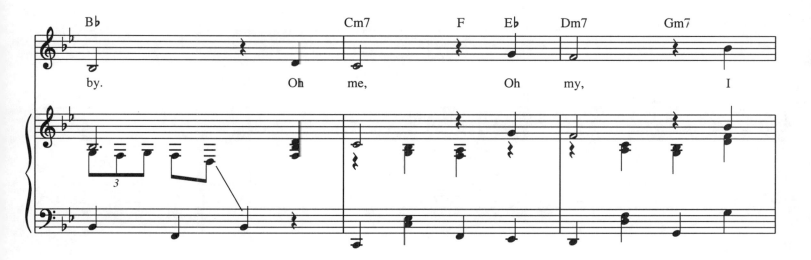

by.   Oh me,   Oh my,   I

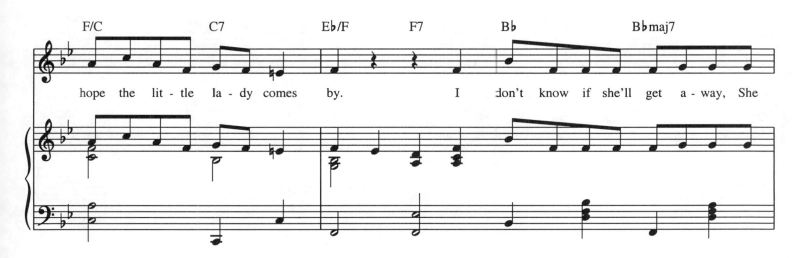

hope the lit-tle la-dy comes by.   I don't know if she'll get a-way, She

doesn't al-ways get a-way, But an-y-way I know that she'll try. Oh

me, Oh my, I hope the lit-tle la-dy comes

by. There's no oth-er girl I could wait for, But

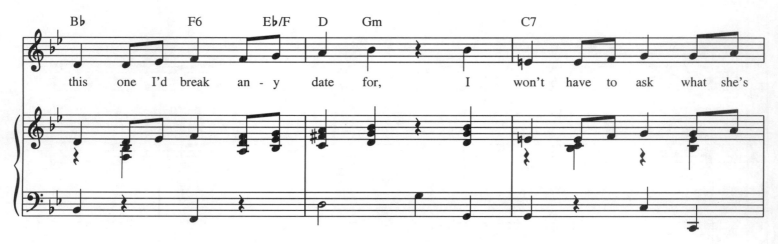

this one I'd break an-y date for, I won't have to ask what she's

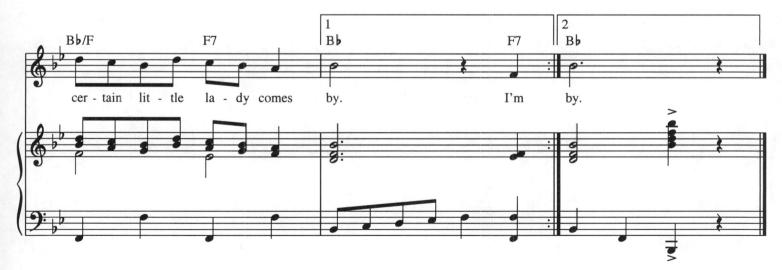

LOSING MY MIND
(From "FOLLIES")

Words and Music by
STEPHEN SONDHEIM

you. And do_ they know?_ It's like I'm los-ing my mind.

Faster

All af - ter - noon, do - ing ev - 'ry lit - tle chore, The thought of you stays

bright. Some-times I stand in the mid-dle of the floor,

Not go - ing left, Not go - ing right. I dim_ the lights And think_ a-bout

you, Spend sleep - less nights To think _ a - bout you. You said _ you loved

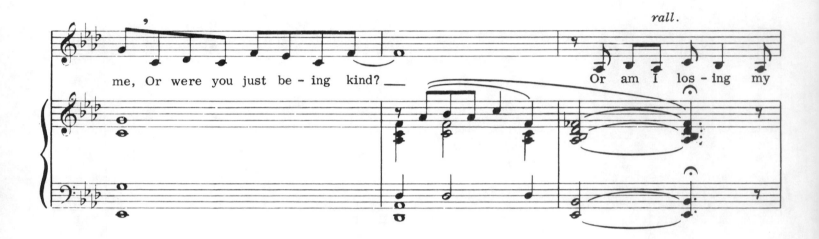

me, Or were you just be - ing kind? _ Or am I los - ing my

mind?

I want _ you so, It's like I'm los - ing my mind. _____

Accelerando

Does no one know? It's like I'm los-ing my mind.

Faster *(colla voce)*

All af-ter-noon, do-ing ev-'ry lit-tle chore, The thought of you stays

bright. Some-times I stand in the mid-dle of the floor,

Not go - ing left, Not go - ing right. I dim _ the lights

And think _ a-bout you, Spend sleep-less nights To think _ a-bout you, You said _ you loved

me Or were you just be-ing kind? Or am I los-ing my

mind?

LOVE, LOOK AWAY

(From "FLOWER DRUM SONG")

Lyrics by OSCAR HAMMERSTEIN II
Music by RICHARD RODGERS

LUCK BE A LADY
(From "GUYS AND DOLLS")

By FRANK LOESSER

Moderately

They call you La-dy Luck but there is room for doubt At

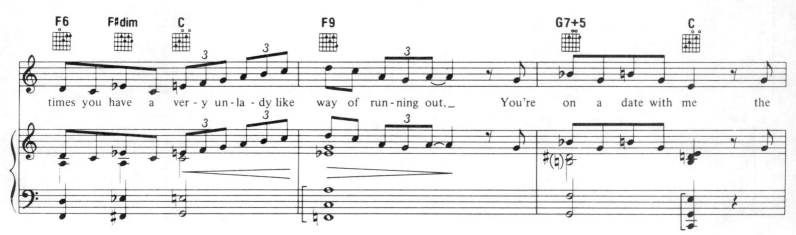

times you have a ver-y un-la-dy like way of run-ning out,_ You're on a date with me the

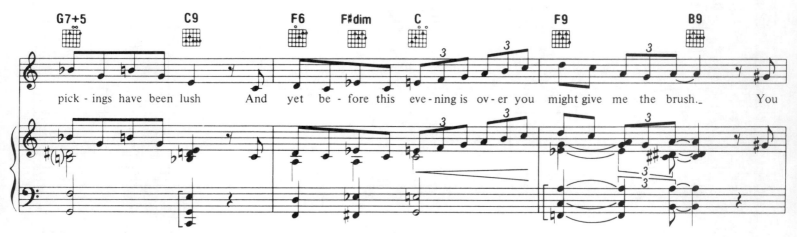

pick-ings have been lush And yet be-fore this eve-ning is ov-er you might give me the brush._ You

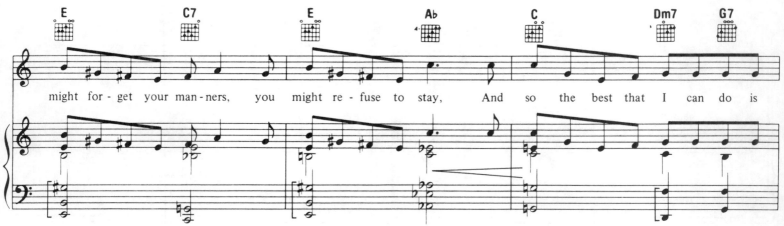

might for-get your man-ners, you might re-fuse to stay, And so the best that I can do is

1

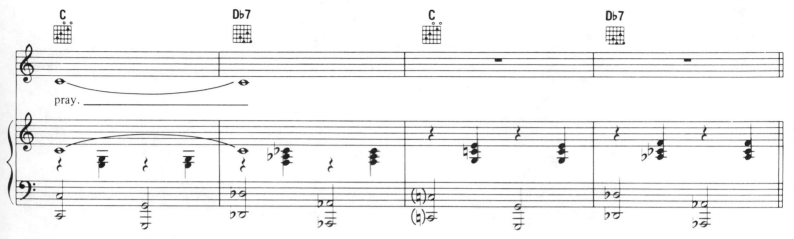

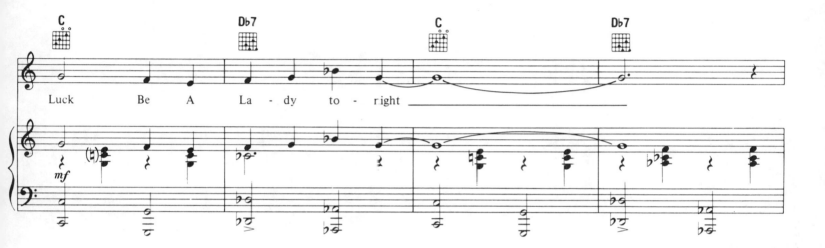

Luck Be A La - dy to - night _____

Luck Be A La - dy to - night _____

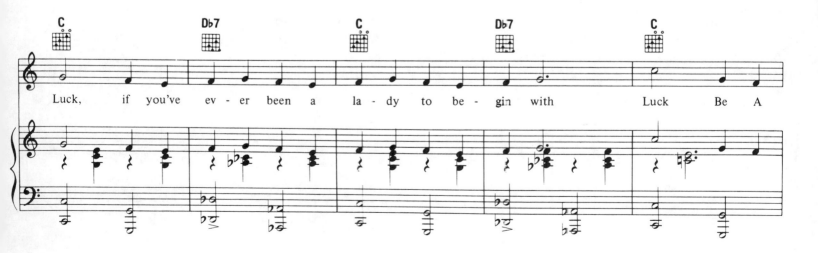

Luck, if you've ev - er been a la - dy to be - gin with   Luck Be A

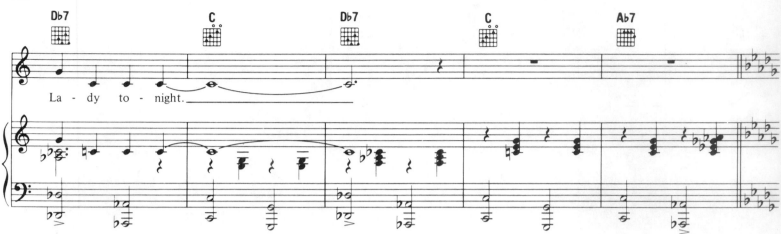

La - dy to - night._____

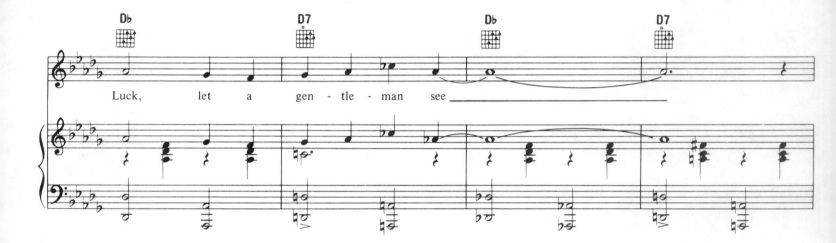

Luck, let a gen - tle - man see _____

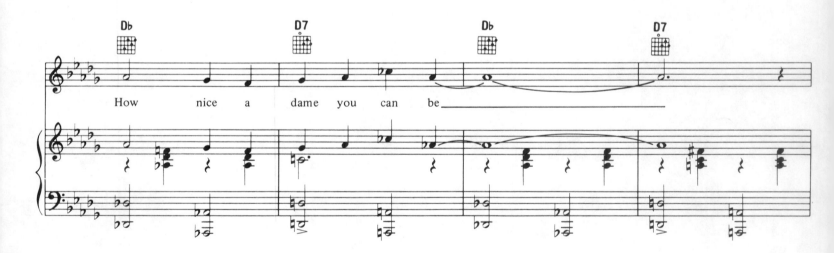

How nice a dame you can be _____

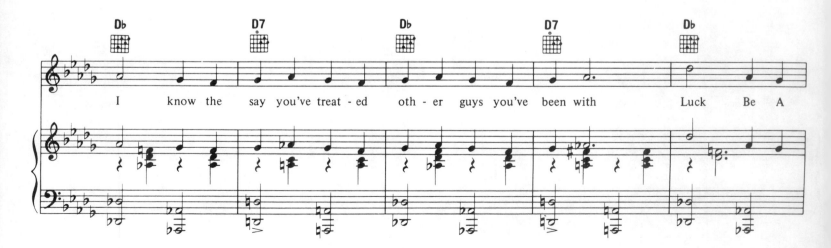

I know the say you've treat - ed oth - er guys you've been with Luck Be A

MAKE UP MY HEART

(From "STARLIGHT EXPRESS")

Music by ANDREW LLOYD WEBBER
Lyrics by RICHARD STILGOE

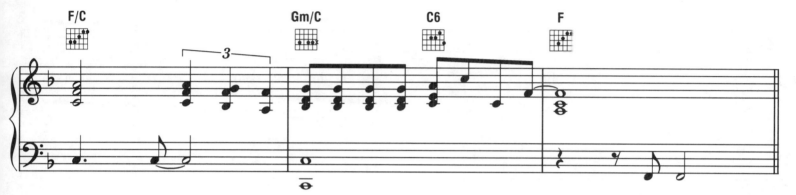

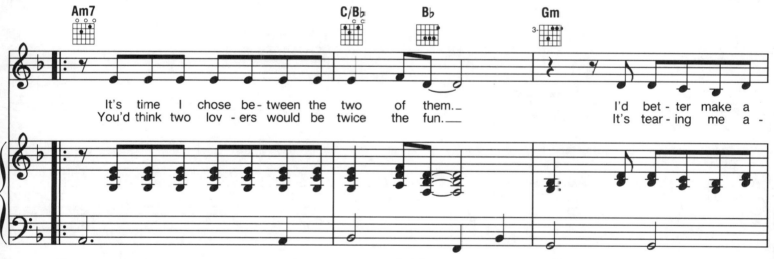

It's time I chose be - tween the two of them.__ I'd bet - ter make a
You'd think two lov - ers would be twice the fun.__ It's tear - ing me a -

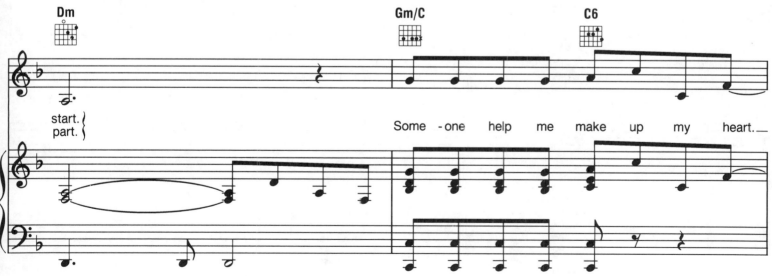

start.
part.

Some - one help me make up my heart.__

174

MAME
(From "MAME")

Music and Lyric by
JERRY HERMAN

With a lilt

You coax the blues right out_ of the horn, Mame,____
You've brought the cake - walk back_ in-to style, Mame,____

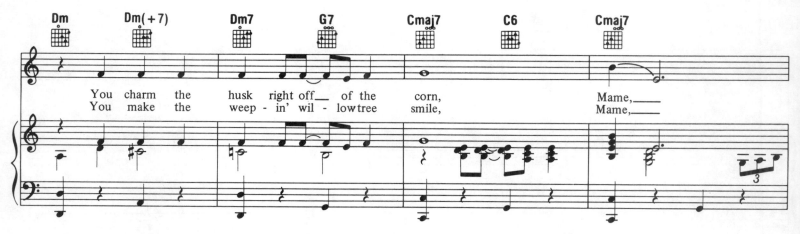

You charm the husk right off__ of the corn, Mame,____
You make the weep - in' wil - lowtree smile, Mame,____

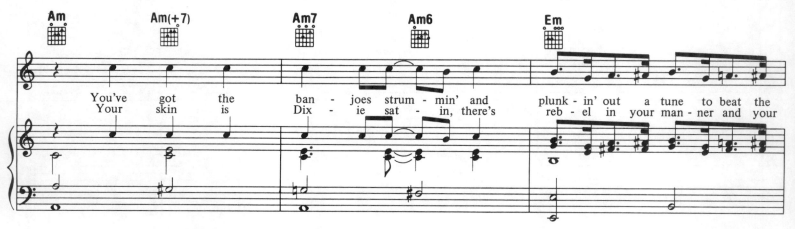

You've got the ban - joes strum - min' and plunk - in' out a tune to beat the
Your skin is Dix - ie sat - in, there's reb - el in your man - ner and your

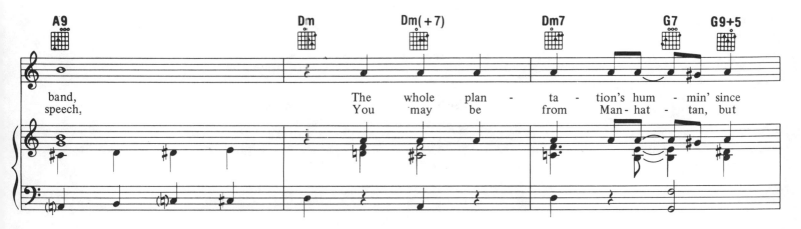

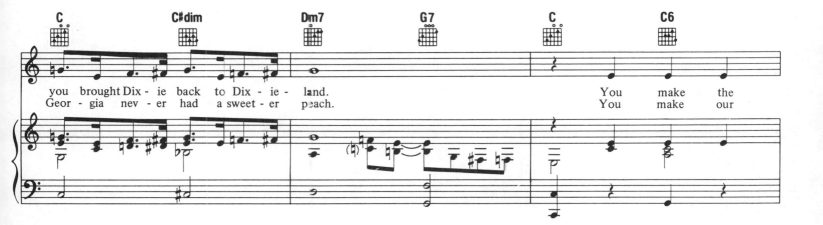

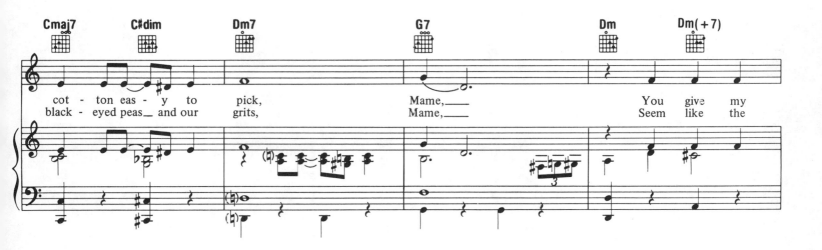

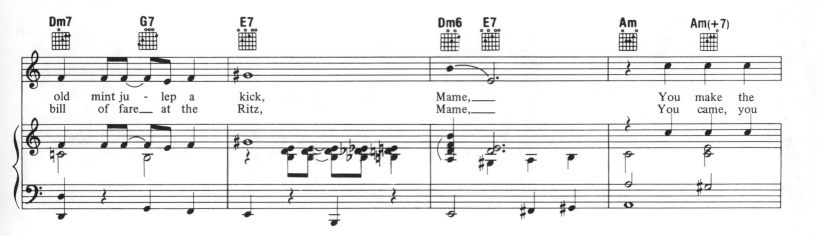

old mag - no - lia tree blos - som at the men - tion of your name,
saw, you con - quered and ab - so - lute - ly noth - ing is the same.

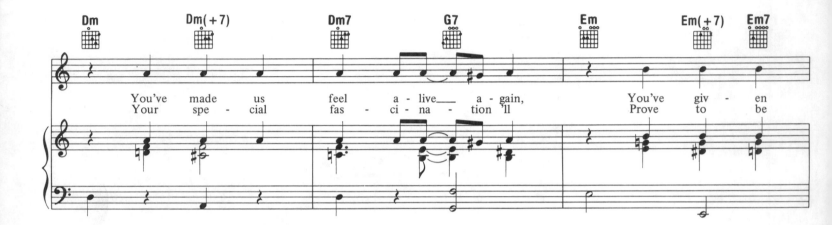

You've made us feel a - live___ a - gain, You've giv - en
Your spe - cial fas - ci - na - tion 'll Prove to be

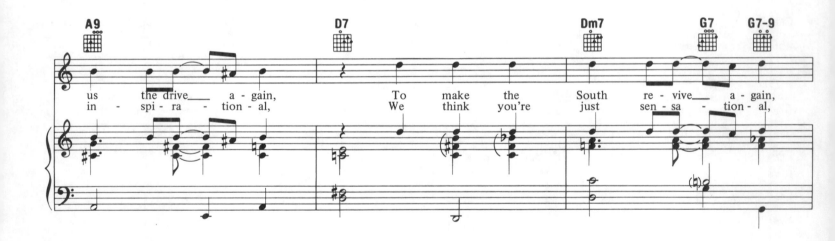

us the drive___ a - gain, To make the South re - vive___ a - gain,
in - spi - ra - tion - al, We think you're just sen - sa - tion - al,

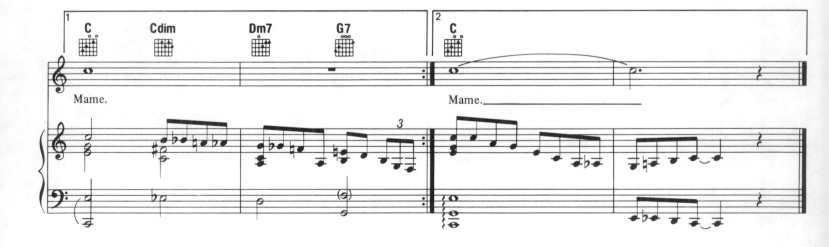

Mame. Mame.___

NEVER NEVER LAND

(From "PETER PAN")

Lyric by BETTY COMDEN and ADOLPH GREEN
Music by JULE STYNE

Moderately

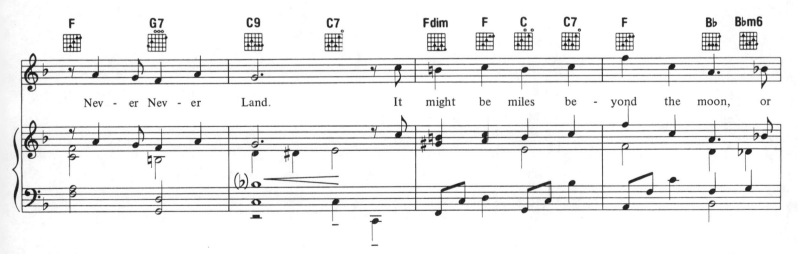

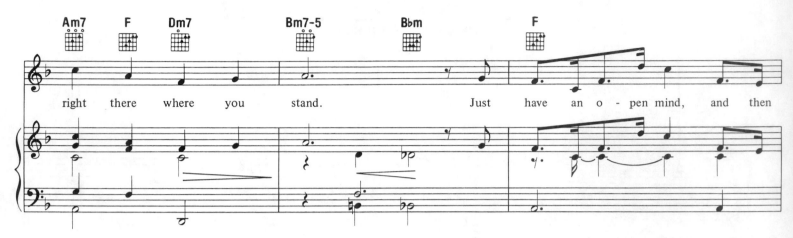

right there where you stand. Just have an o-pen mind, and then

sud-den-ly you'll find Nev-er Nev-er Land. You'll have a treas-ure if you

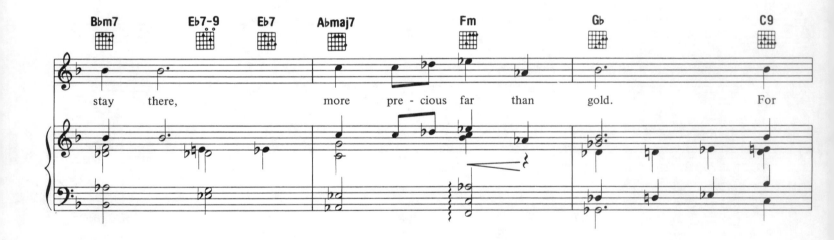

stay there, more pre-cious far than gold. For

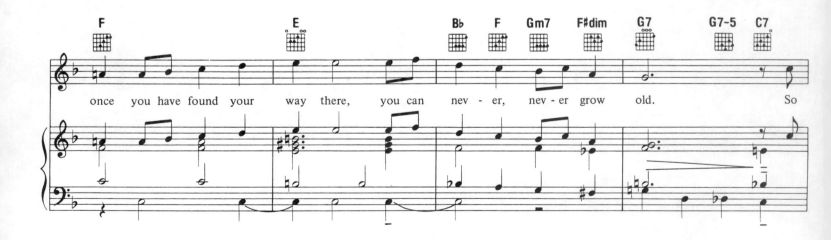

once you have found your way there, you can nev-er, nev-er grow old. So

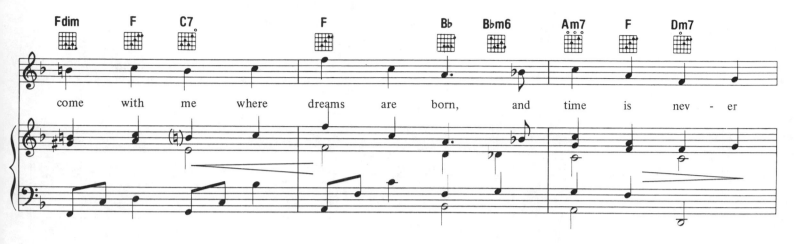

come with me where dreams are born, and time is nev - er

planned.   Just think of love - ly things, and your heart will fly on wings, for

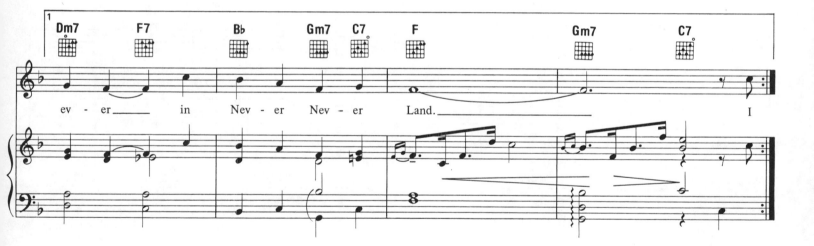

ev - er____ in Nev - er Nev - er Land._____   I

ev - er____ in Nev - er Nev - er Land._____

MAYBE THIS TIME
(From The Musical "CABARET")

Words by FRED EBB
Music by JOHN KANDER

185

MEMORY
(From "CATS")

Music by ANDREW LLOYD WEBBER
Text by TREVOR NUNN after T.S. ELIOT

Mid - night.___ Not a sound from the pave - ment. Has the moon lost her

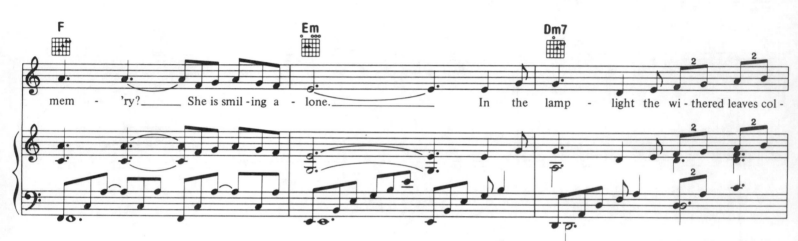

mem - 'ry?___ She is smil - ing a - lone.___ In the lamp - light the wi - thered leaves col -

lect at my feet___ And the wind___ be - gins to moan.

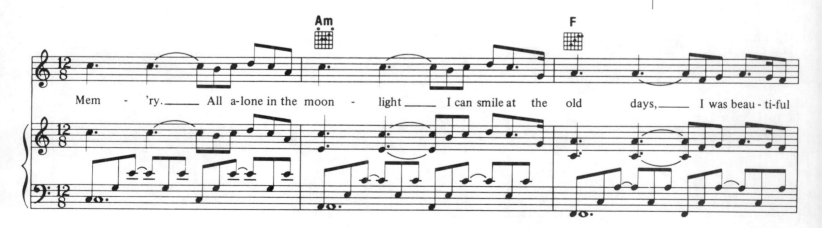

Mem - 'ry.___ All a-lone in the moon - light___ I can smile at the old days,___ I was beau - ti - ful

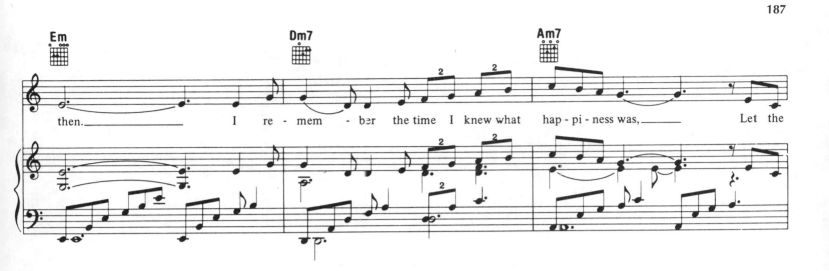

then._____ I re - mem - ber the time I knew what hap - pi - ness was,_____ Let the

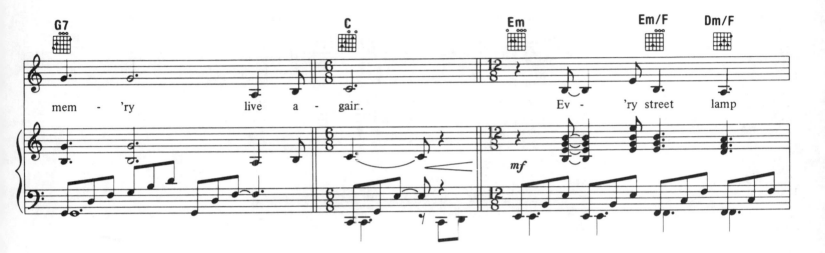

mem - 'ry live a - gain. Ev - 'ry street lamp

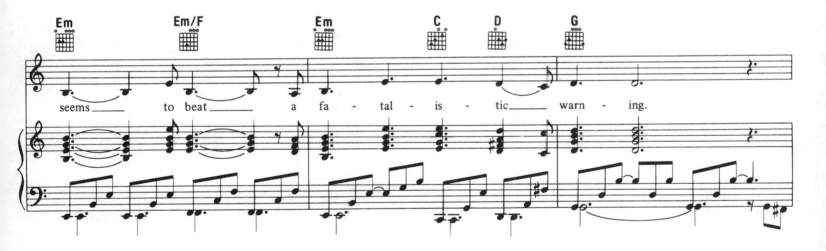

seems_____ to beat_____ a fa - tal - is - tic_____ warn - ing.

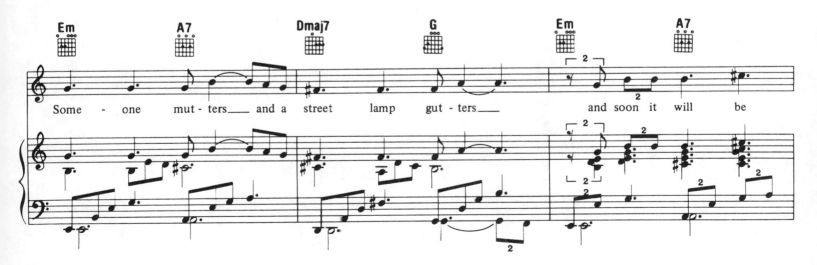

Some - one mut - ters_____ and a street lamp gut - ters_____ and soon it will be

MY HEART STOOD STILL
(From "A CONNECTICUT YANKEE")

Words by LORENZ HART
Music by RICHARD RODGERS

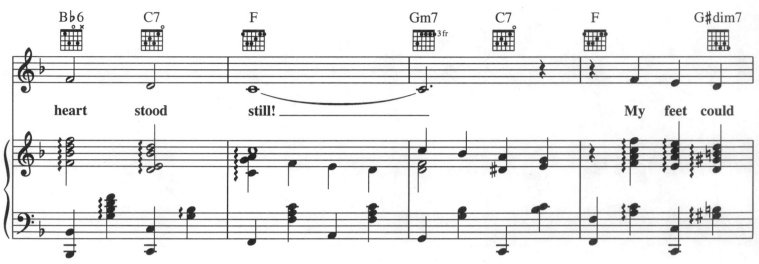

heart stood still! _____ My feet could

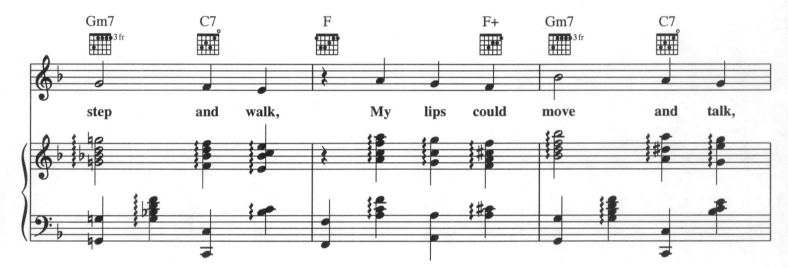

step and walk, My lips could move and talk,

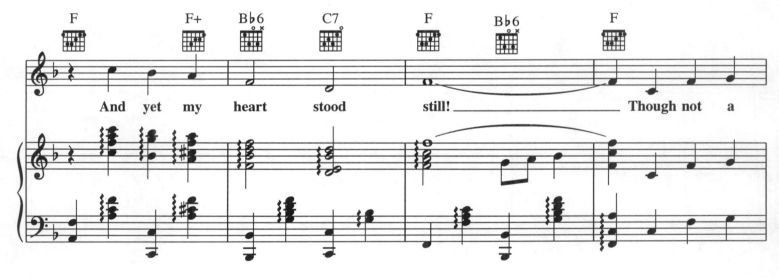

And yet my heart stood still! _____ Though not a

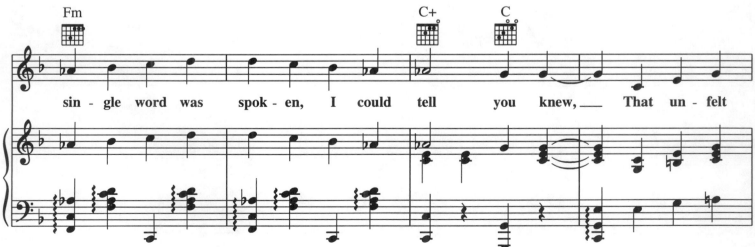

sin - gle word was spok - en, I could tell you knew, ___ That un - felt

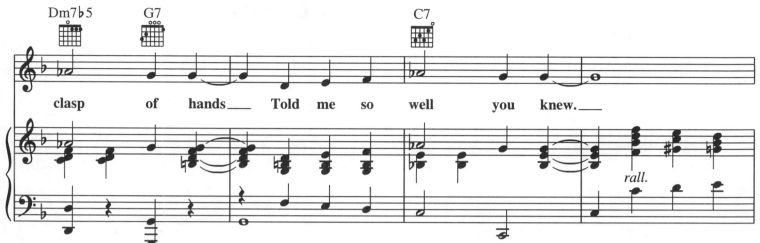

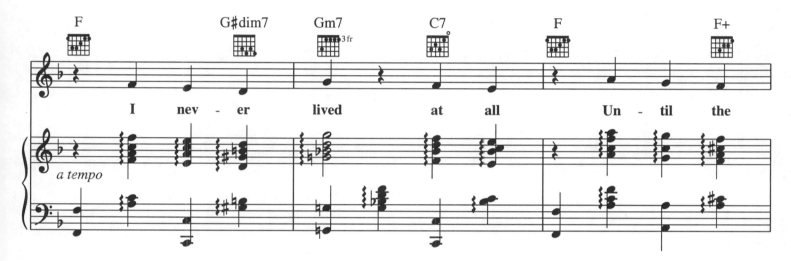

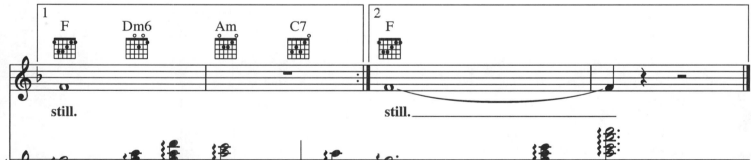

NO OTHER LOVE

(From "ME AND JULIET")

Lyrics by OSCAR HAMMERSTEIN II
Music by RICHARD RODGERS

Refrain *(slow Tango tempo)*

OKLAHOMA
(From "OKLAHOMA!")

Lyrics by OSCAR HAMMERSTEIN II
Music by RICHARD RODGERS

ONE
(From "A CHORUS LINE")

Music by MARVIN HAMLISCH
Lyric by EDWARD KLEBAN

Moderately

Ebmaj7 · **A7** · **Ebmaj7** · **Gm7-5** · **C7**

One sin-gu-lar sen-sa-tion ev-'ry lit-tle step she takes,— One thrill-ing com-bi-na-tion Ev-'ry move that she makes.

SEASONS OF LOVE
(From "RENT")

Words and Music by
JONATHAN LARSON

Five hun-dred twen-ty five thou-sand six hun-dred min - utes,

five hun-dred twen-ty five thou-sand mo-ments so __ dear.__ Five hun-dred twen-ty five thou-sand

six hun - dred min - utes. How do you meas-ure, meas-ure a __ year?__ In

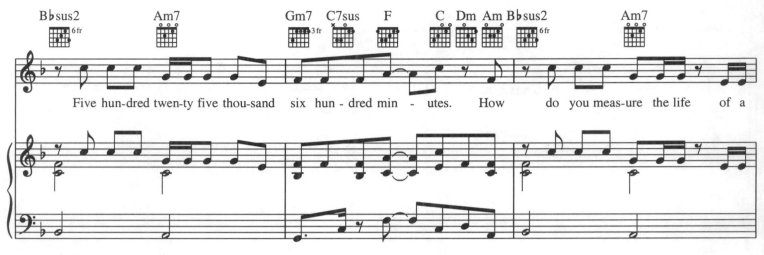

Five hun-dred twen-ty five thou-sand six hun-dred min - utes. How do you meas-ure the life of a

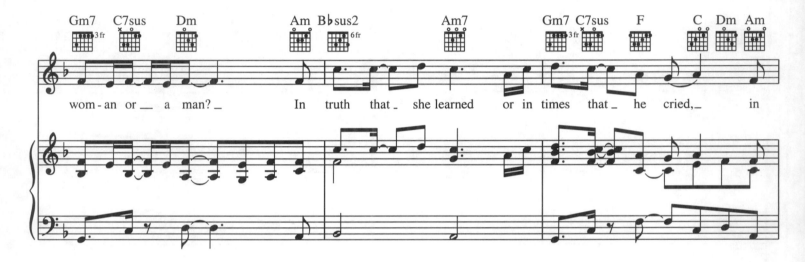

wom-an or __ a man? __ In truth that _ she learned or in times that _ he cried, __ in

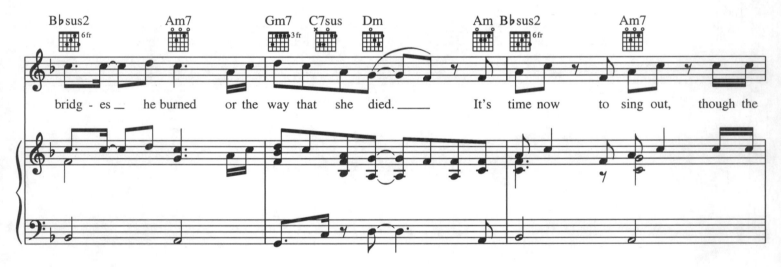

bridg - es __ he burned or the way that she died. ____ It's time now to sing out, though the

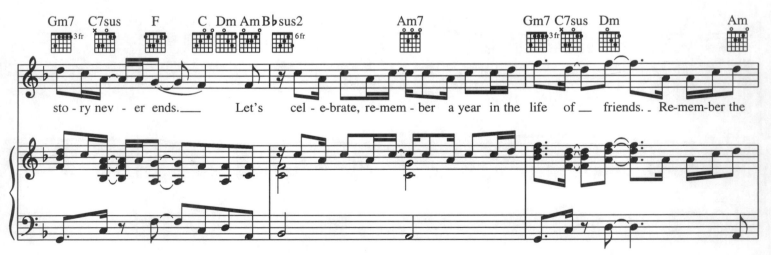

sto - ry nev - er ends. ___ Let's cel - e-brate, re-mem - ber a year in the life of __ friends. _ Re-mem-ber the

PEOPLE
(From "FUNNY GIRL")

Words by BOB MERRILL
Music by JULE STYNE

Moderately

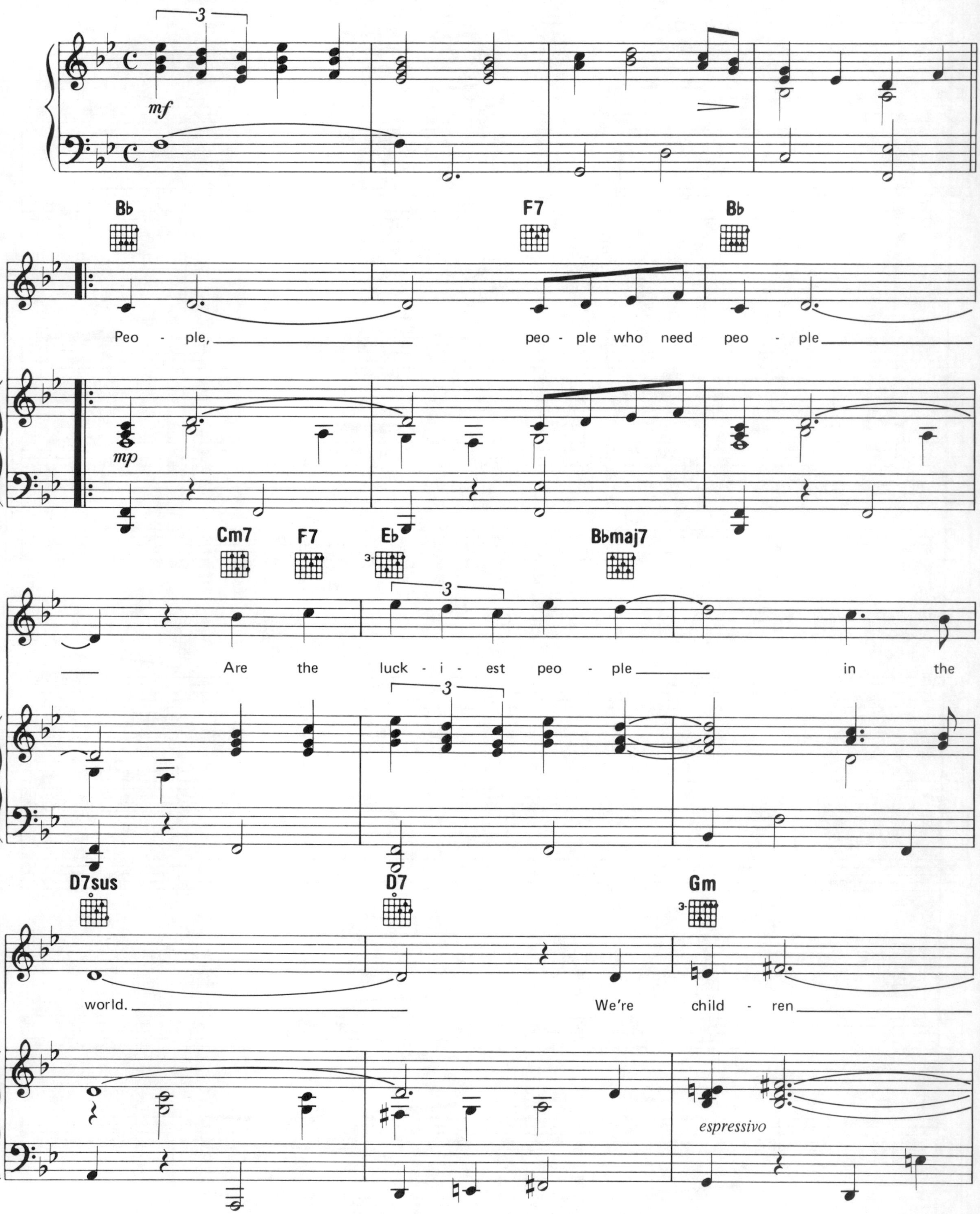

mf
Bb
F7
Bb
Peo - ple,
peo - ple who need peo - ple
mp
Cm7
F7
Eb
Bbmaj7
Are the luck - i - est peo - ple in the
D7sus
D7
Gm
world.
We're child - ren
espressivo

SHADOWLAND

(Disney Presents "THE LION KING: THE BROADWAY MUSICAL")

Music by HANS ZIMMER and LEBO M
Lyrics by MARK MANCINA and LEBO M

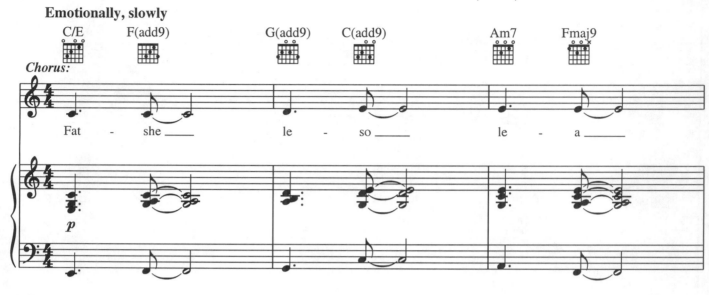

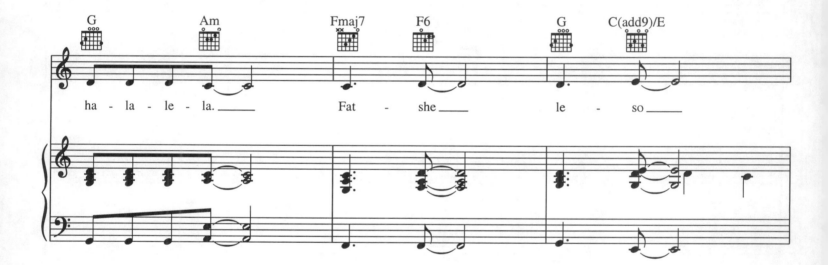

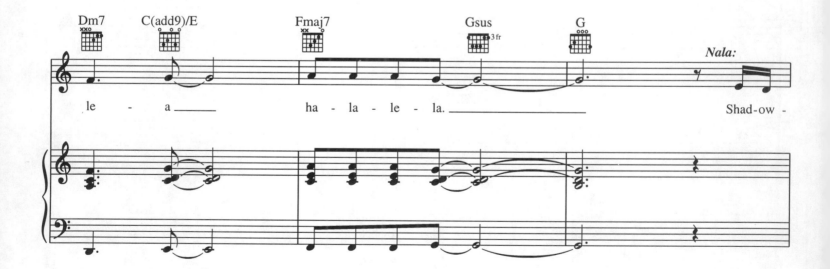

land, _____ the leaves ___ have

fall - en. _____ This shad - owed

land, _____ this was our

home. The _____ riv - er's

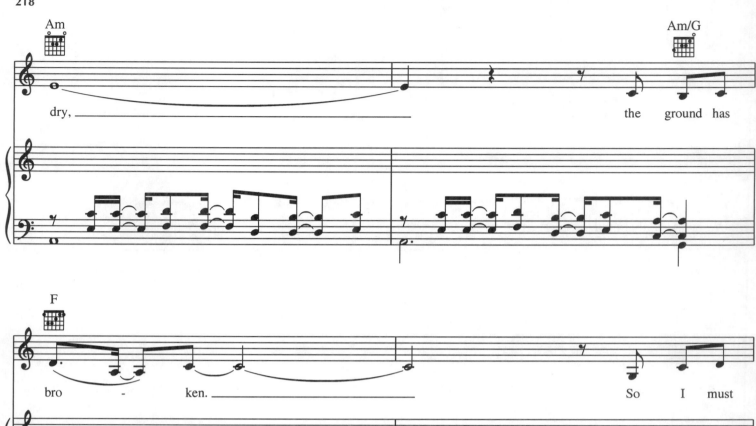

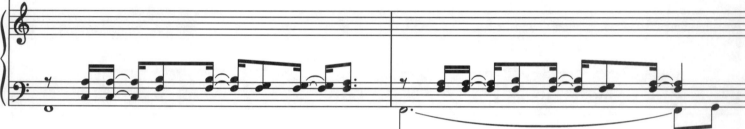

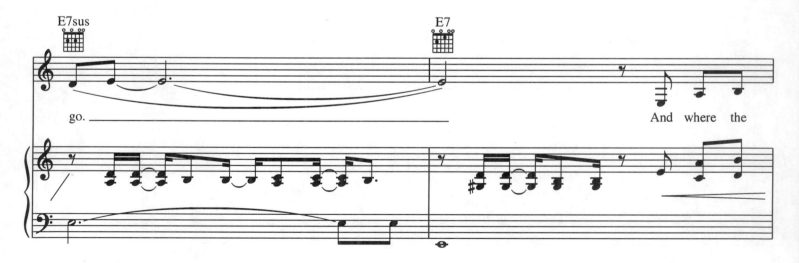

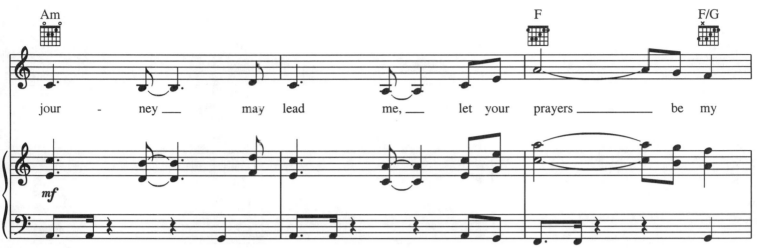

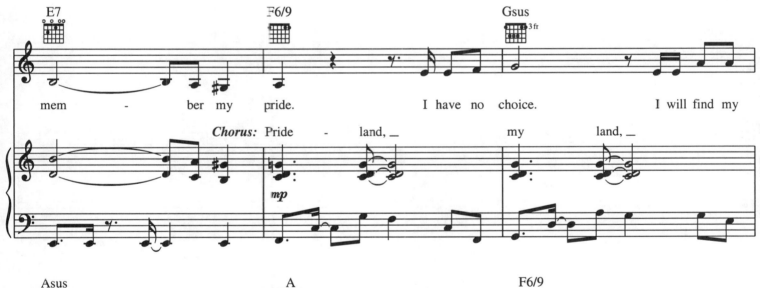

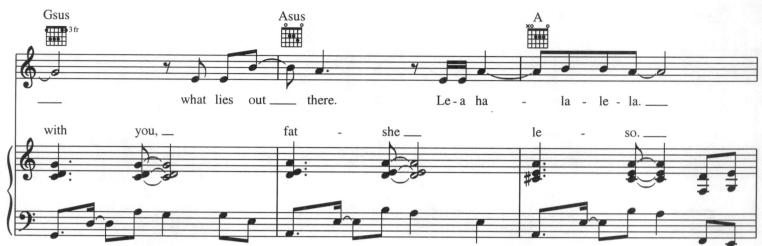

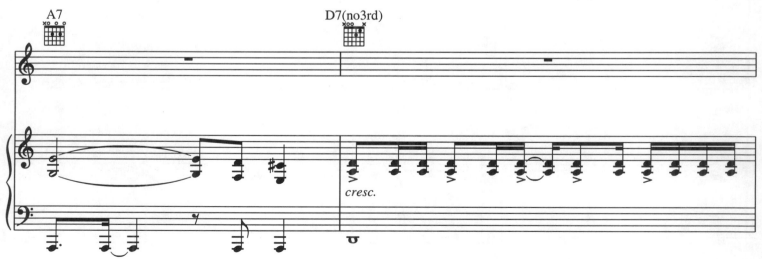

222

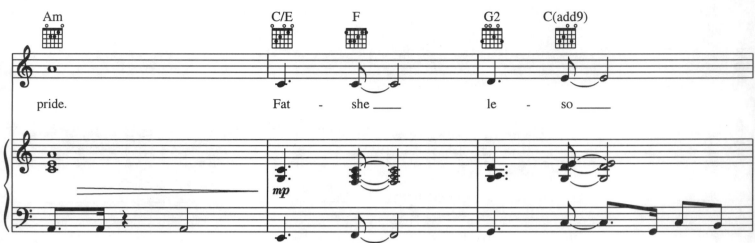

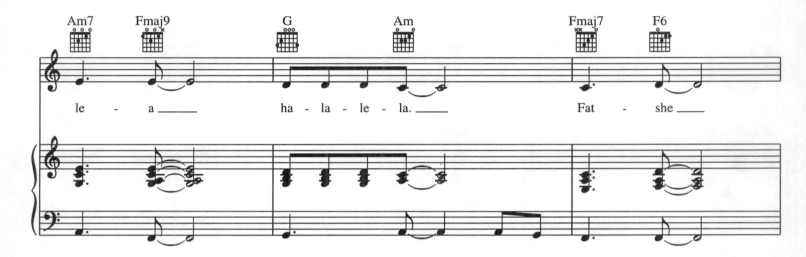

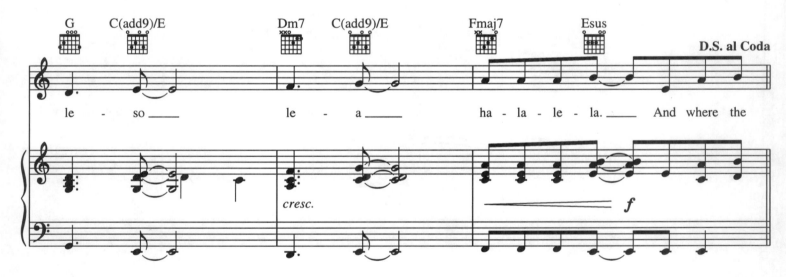

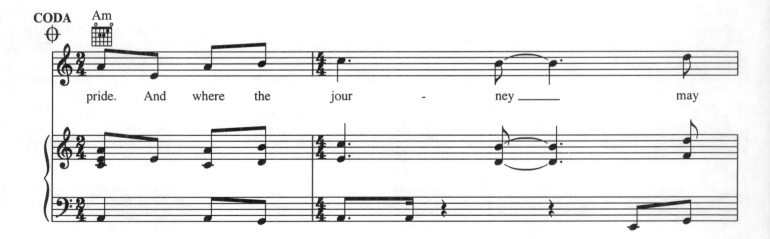

SOME ENCHANTED EVENING
(From "SOUTH PACIFIC")

Lyrics by OSCAR HAMMERSTEIN II
Music by RICHARD RODGERS

You may hear her laugh - ing _____ A - cross a crowd - ed room

And night af - ter night, _____ As strange as it seems, _____

The sound of her laugh - ter will sing in your dreams. _____

Who can ex - plain it? Who can tell you why?

227

side _____ And make her your own, _____ Or all through your

life you may dream all a - lone. _____

Once you have found her, Nev - er let her go. Once you have found her,

Nev - er let her go! _____

SOMEONE ELSE'S STORY
(From "CHESS")

Words and Music by
BENNY ANDERSSON, TIM RICE
and BJORN ULVAEUS

Slow 8 - Beat Ballad

would he lis-ten if __ I stay?__ All ver-y well to say you

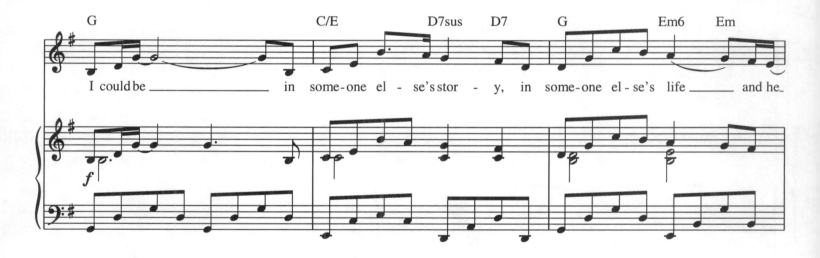

fool it's now or nev - er. I could be choos - ing no choi-ces what-so-ev-er.

I could be _____ in some-one el - se's stor - y, in some-one el - se's life _____ and he_

__ could be in mine._ I don't see _____ a rea-son to be lone - ly.

SOMEBODY'S EYES
(From The Broadway Musical "FOOTLOOSE")

Words by DEAN PITCHFORD
Music by TOM SNOW

Tense and precise

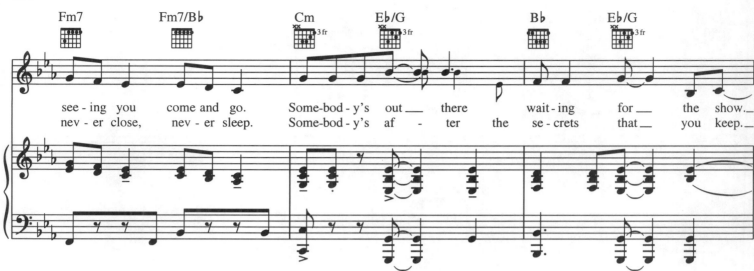

see - ing you come and go. Some-bod - y's out __ there wait - ing for __ the show. __
nev - er close, nev - er sleep. Some-bod - y's af - ter the se - crets that __ you keep. __

You've got no dis-guise from some-bod - y's eyes. __
Who's got al - i - bis from some-bod - y's eyes? __

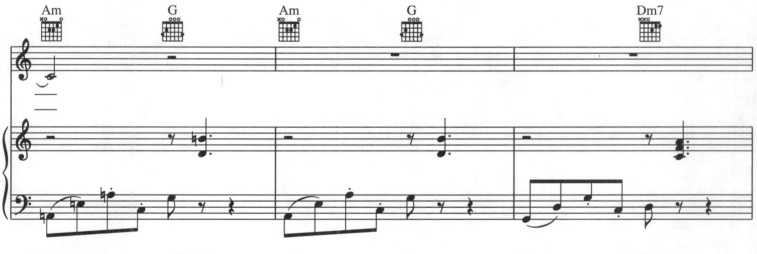

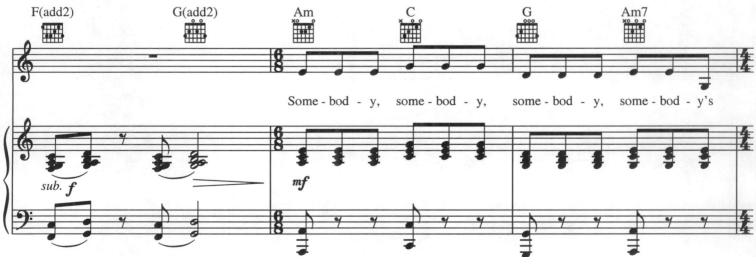

Some - bod - y, some - bod - y, some - bod - y, some - bod - y's

237

naugh - ty thought, _ and if you get caught, _ well then,

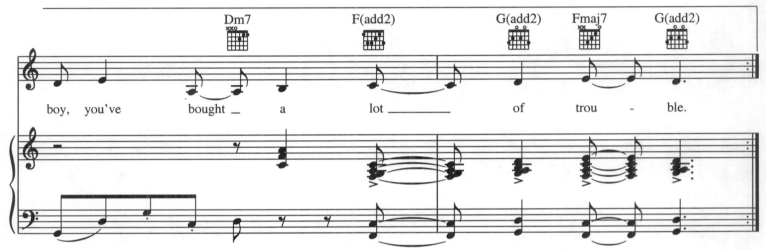

boy, you've bought _ a lot _____ of trou - ble.

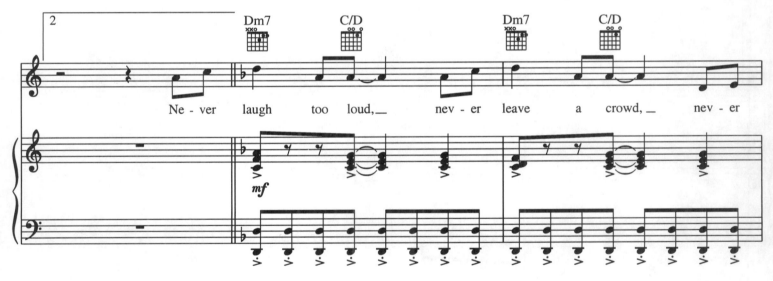

Ne - ver laugh too loud, _ nev - er leave a crowd, _ nev - er

dress ris - qué, _____ there'll be hell to pay. _____ If you've

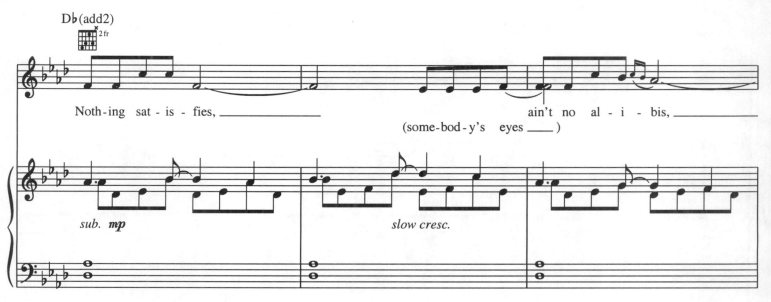

Noth-ing sat - is - fies, _____ ain't no al - i - bis, _____
(some-bod-y's eyes ___)

sub. *mp*   *slow cresc.*

_____ you've got no dis - guise_____ from some-bod-y's eyes,_
(in some-bod-y's eyes ___)

f

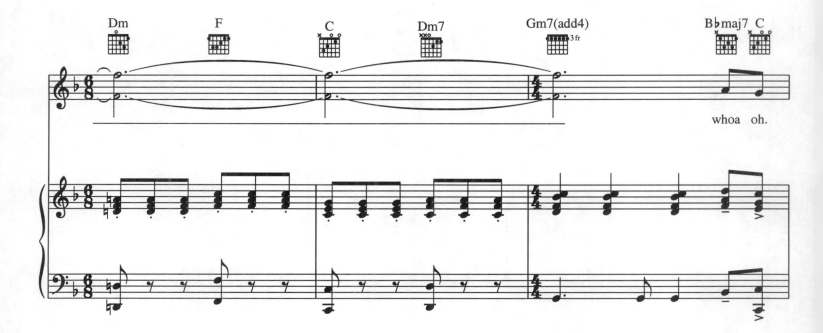

whoa oh.

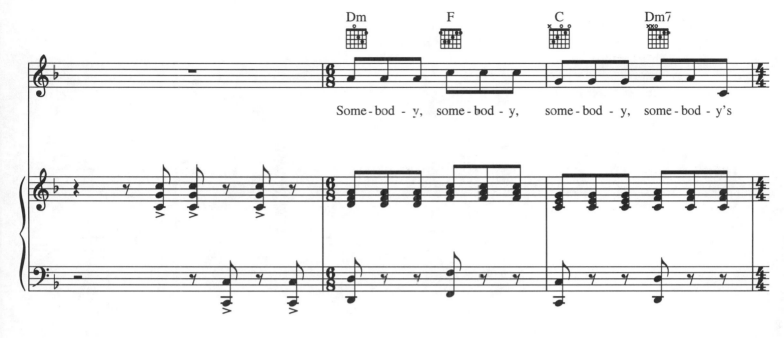

Some-bod - y, some-bod - y, some-bod - y, some-bod - y's

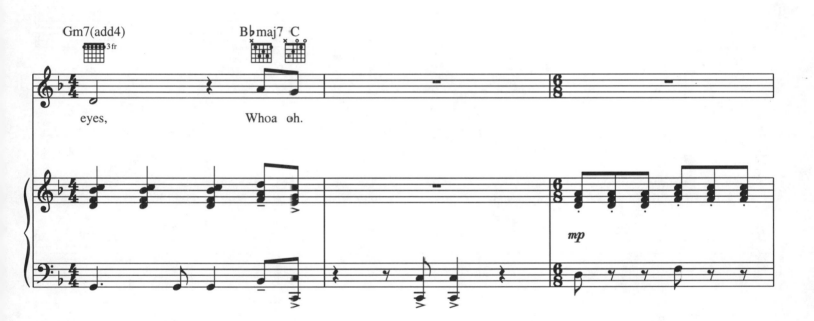

eyes, Whoa oh.

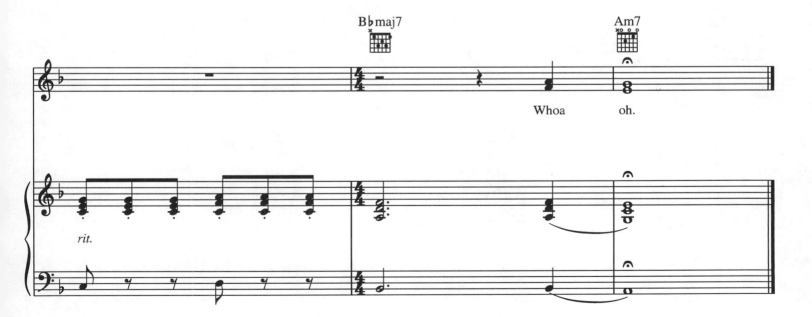

Whoa oh.

SOMEONE LIKE YOU

(From "JEKYLL & HYDE")

Words by LESLIE BRICUSSE
Music by FRANK WILDHORN

243

245

STAYIN' ALIVE
(From "SATURDAY NIGHT FEVER")

Words and Music by BARRY GIBB,
MAURICE GIBB and ROBIN GIBB

Medium Rock beat

Well, you can tell

— by the way I use— my walk,— I'm a wom - an's man; no time to talk..

— get low and I get high,— and if I— can't get ei - ther, I real - ly try.— Got the

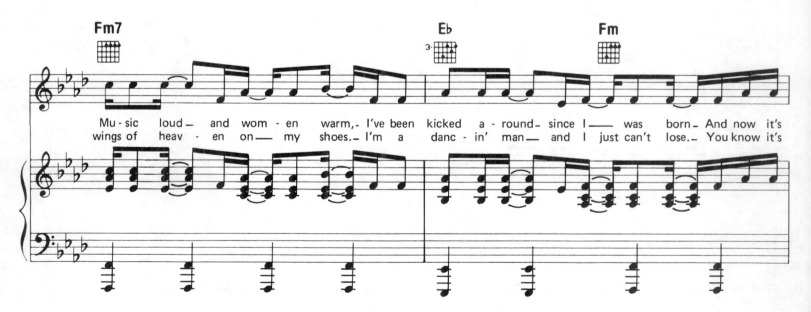

Mu - sic loud— and wom - en warm,— I've been kicked a - round— since I— was born. And now it's

wings of heav - en on— my shoes.. I'm a danc - in' man— and I just can't lose.— You know it's

248

Some-bod-y help me. ____ Some-bod-y help__ me, yeah.__

Fm7

Bb7

____ Life go-in' no - where.__

Fm7

Some-bod-y help__ me, yeah.__ I'm stay-in' a - live..

Repeat and Fade

THE SWEETEST SOUNDS
(From "NO STRINGS")

Lyrics and Music by
RICHARD RODGERS

SUPPER TIME
(From The Stage Production "AS THOUSANDS CHEER")

Words and Music by
IRVING BERLIN

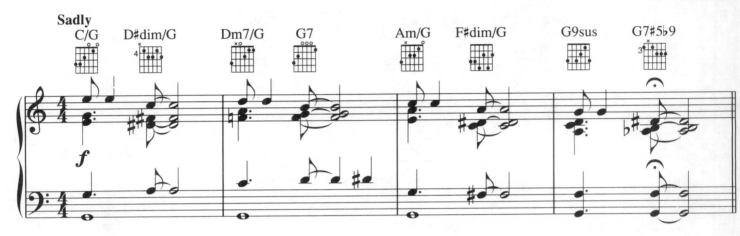

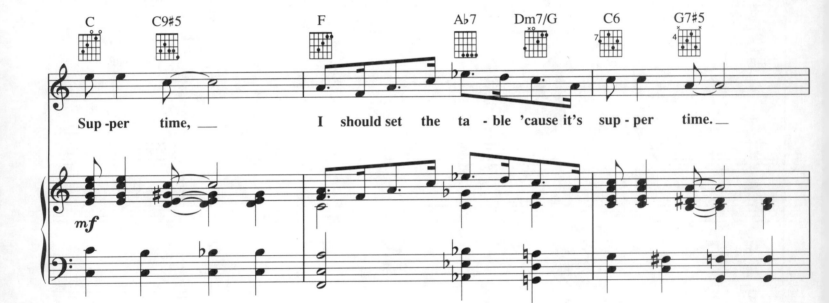

Sup-per time, ___ I should set the ta-ble 'cause it's sup-per time. ___

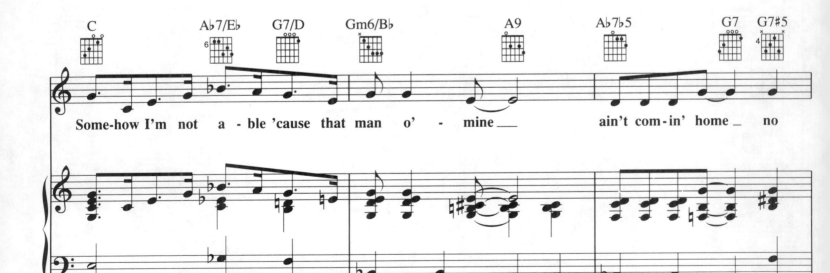

Some-how I'm not a - ble 'cause that man o' - mine ___ ain't com-in' home ___ no

TELL ME ON A SUNDAY

(From "SONG & DANCE")

Music by ANDREW LLOYD WEBBER
Lyrics by DON BLACK

TEN CENTS A DANCE
(From "SIMPLE SIMON")

Words by LORENZ HART
Music by RICHARD RODGERS

I work at the Pal-ace Ball-room, but, gee, that pal-ace is cheap. When I get back to my chill-y hall room I'm much too ti-red to sleep. I'm one of those la-dy teach-ers, a beau-ti-ful host-ess, you

8vb

THERE IS NOTHIN' LIKE A DAME
(From "SOUTH PACIFIC")

Lyrics by OSCAR HAMMERSTEIN II
Music by RICHARD RODGERS

We got sun-light on the sand, We got moon-light on the sea, We got

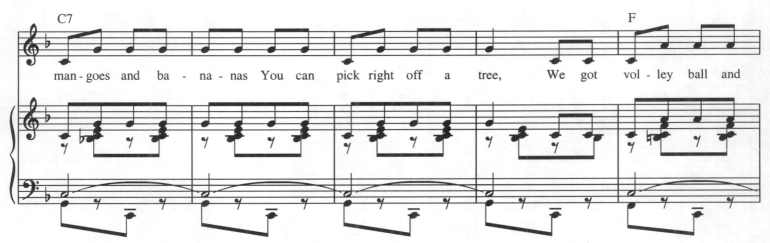

man-goes and ba-na-nas You can pick right off a tree, We got vol-ley ball and

ping pong And a lot of dan-dy games! What ain't we got? We

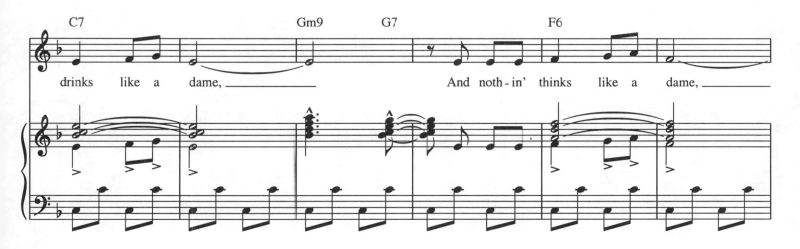

THERE'S A SMALL HOTEL
(From "ON YOUR TOES")

Words by LORENZ HART
Music by RICHARD RODGERS

Moderately

poco rit.

There's a small ho-tel With a wish-ing well; I wish that we were there to-geth - er. _____

There's a brid-al suite; One room bright and neat, Com-

THEY LIVE IN YOU
(Disney Presents "THE LION KING: THE BROADWAY MUSICAL")

Music and Lyrics by MARK MANCINA,
JAY RIFKIN and LEBO M

Spiritually, steadily

In - gon-ya - ma nengw' en - a - ma-ba - la.

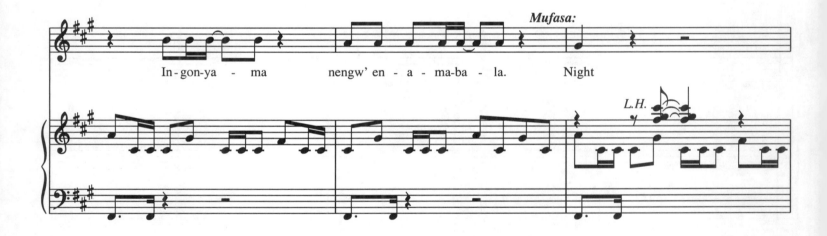

In - gon-ya - ma nengw' en - a - ma-ba - la. Night

and the spir - it __ of life call - ing.

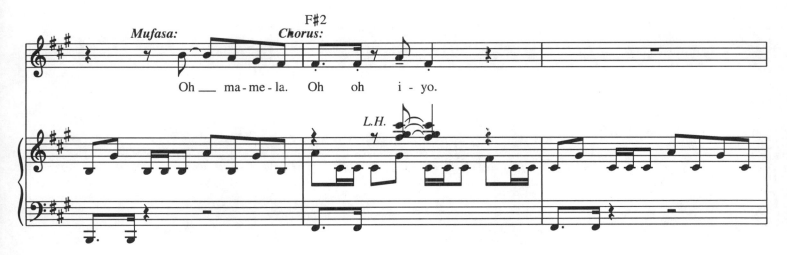

Chorus:

Ma-me - la ma-me-la iyo. He - la.

Mufasa: F#2

Wait, there's no moun-tain too great.

B2

Hear these words and have ___ faith. Oh ___

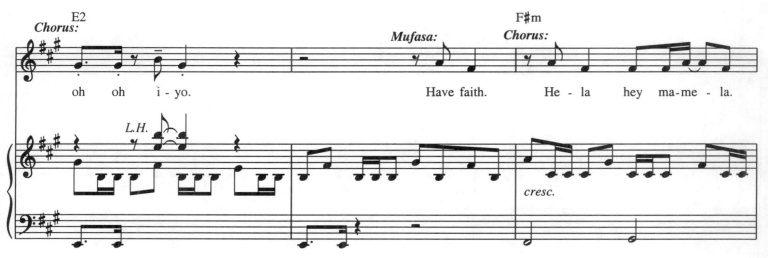

E2

Chorus:

oh oh i - yo.

Mufasa: Have faith.

Chorus: F#m

He - la hey ma-me - la.

cresc.

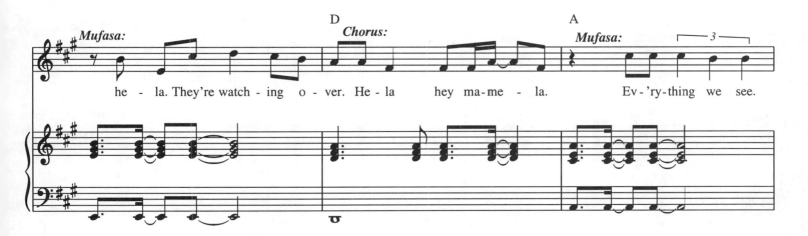

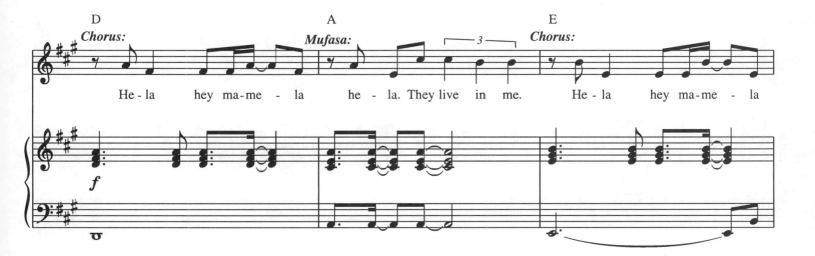

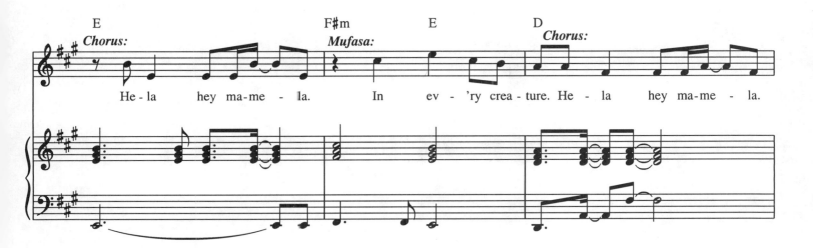

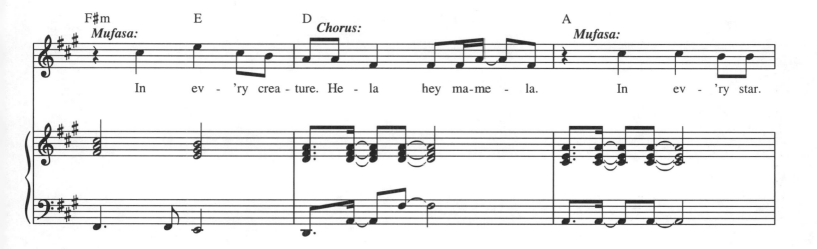

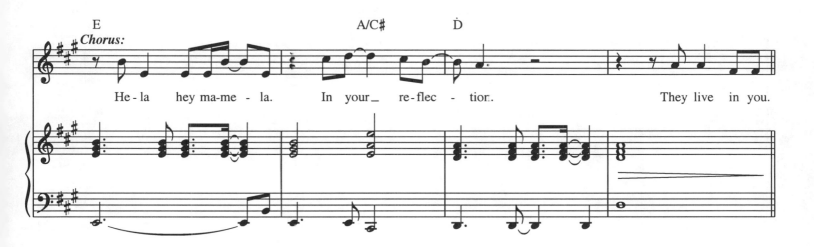

THIS IS THE MOMENT
(From "JEKYLL & HYDE")

Words by LESLIE BRICUSSE
Music by FRANK WILDHORN

F#m7   E/G#   A   B7sus4

com-ing____ in-to play,   is   here and now__ to-day._____   This is the

F#m7/B   Emaj7   F#m7/B

mo-ment,_____   this is the time   when the mo-men-tum   and the mo-ment   are in

Emaj7   C#madd2   G#m

rhyme.   Give me this mo-ment,_____   this__ pre-cious chance.   I'll

F#m7   E/G#   A   A/B   B7

gath-er____ up my past   and   make some sense_ at   last.   This is the

% E F#m7/E E. F#m7b5/E

mo - ment when all I've done, all of the
mo - ment, my fi - nal test. Des - ti - ny

E C#m Amaj7 B/A

dream - ing, schem - ing and scream - ing be - come one! This is the
beck - oned, I nev - er reck - oned sec - ond best. I won't look

F#m7 B/A G#m7 C#m *To Coda*

day, see it spar - kle and shine, when all I've
down, I must not fall. This is the

F#m7 F#m7/B E Esus4 B/A A G#m7 E/G#

lived for_____ be - comes mine! For all these years I've

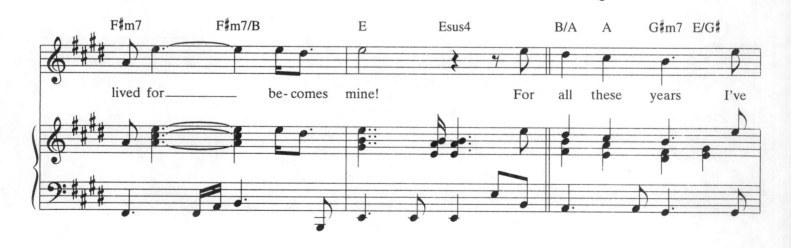

TILL THERE WAS YOU
(From Meredith Willson's "THE MUSIC MAN")

By MEREDITH WILLSON

Moderately

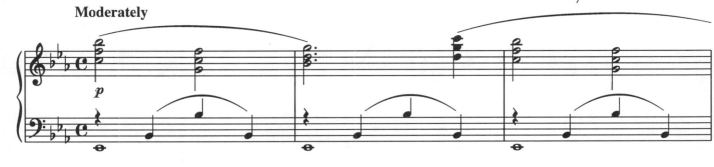

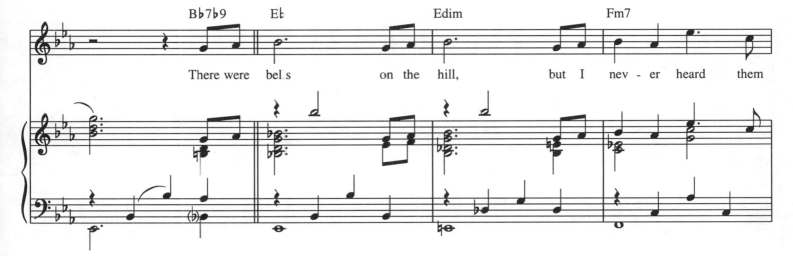

There were bells on the hill, but I nev-er heard them

ring - ing, No, I nev - er heard them at all till there was

you._____ There were birds in the sky, but I

never saw them wing - ing, No, I nev - er saw them at

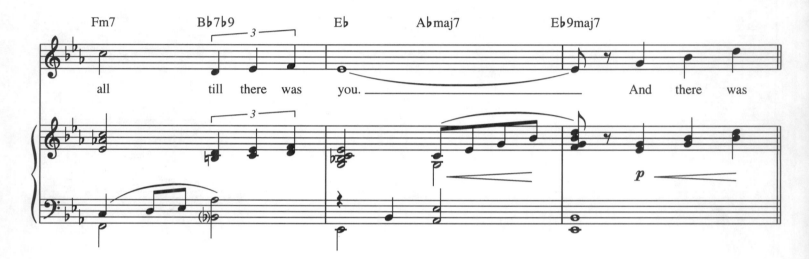

all till there was you. _____ And there was

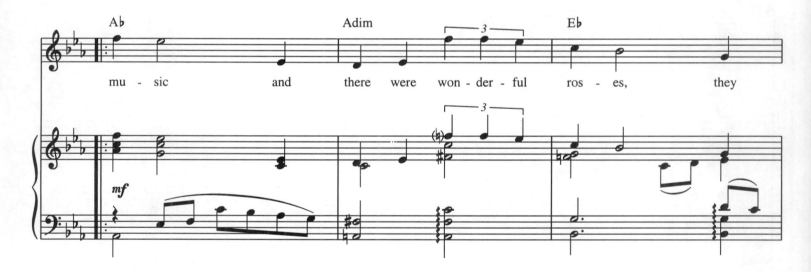

mu - sic and there were won - der - ful ros - es, they

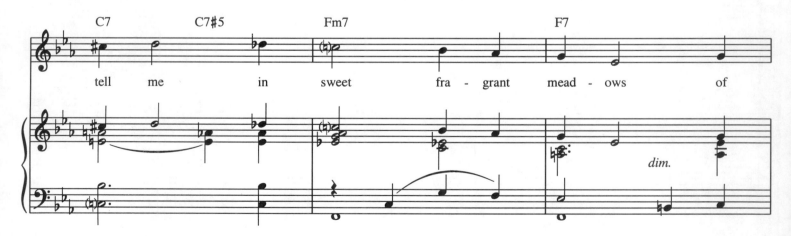

tell me in sweet fra - grant mead - ows of

dawn, and dew, There was love all a-

round, but I nev-er heard it sing-ing, No, I

nev-er heard it at all till there was you.

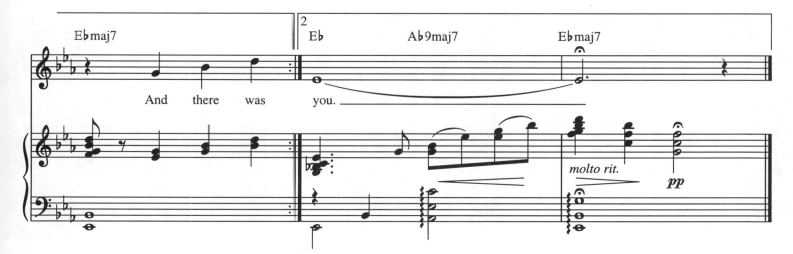

And there was you. _____

THOU SWELL
(From "A CONNECTICUT YANKEE")

Words by LORENZ HART
Music by RICHARD RODGERS

sweet! Thou grand! Wouldst kiss me pret-ty? _____ Wouldst

hold my hand? Both thine eyes __ are cute, too; What they do to

me. _____ Hear me hol-ler I choose a Sweet lol-la - pa-loo-sa in

thee. _____ I'd feel so rich in _____ a

TOMORROW
(From The Musical Production "ANNIE")

Lyric by MARTIN CHARNIN
Music by CHARLES STROUSE

Moderately slow

The sun-'ll come out _____ to-mor-row,

bet your bot-tom dol-lar that to-mor-row _____ there'll be

sun! Jus' think-ing a-bout _____ to-mor-row

296

UNUSUAL WAY
(IN A VERY UNUSUAL WAY)
(From "NINE")

Words and Music by
MAURY YESTON

Flowing (♪=84)

In a

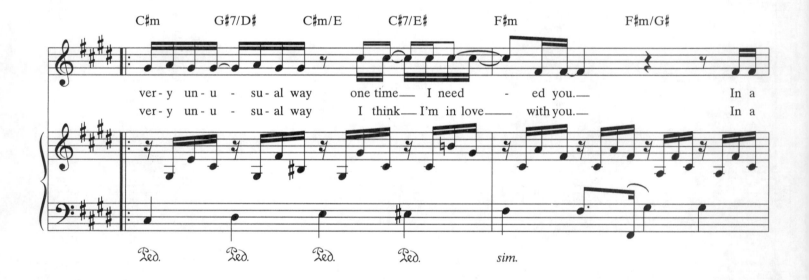

ver-y un-u-su-al way   one time— I need   -ed you.—   In a
ver-y un-u-su-al way   I think— I'm in love—   with you.—   In a

ver-y un-u-su-al way   you were— my— friend.
ver-y un-u-su-al way   I want— to— cry.

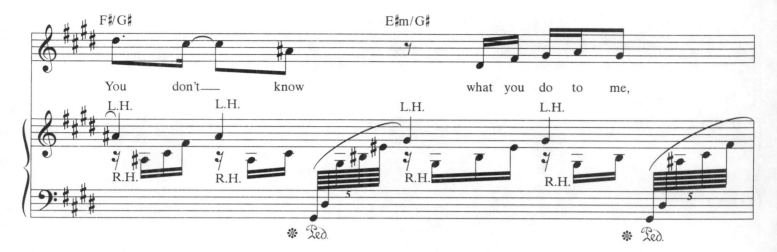

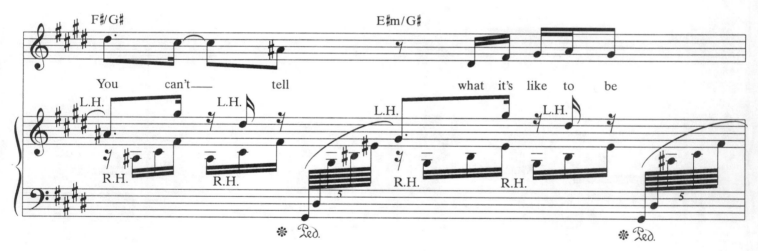

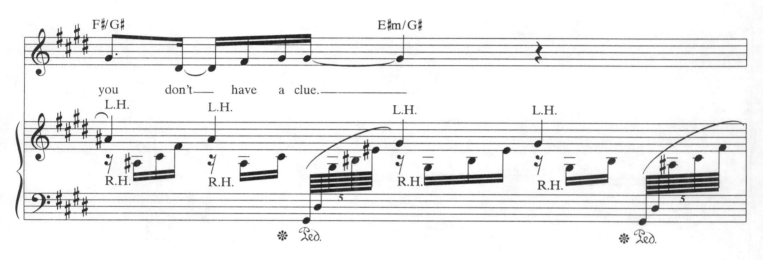

how could I ev - er for-get— you once— you had touched— my soul?—

In   a   ver-y un-u - su-al way———

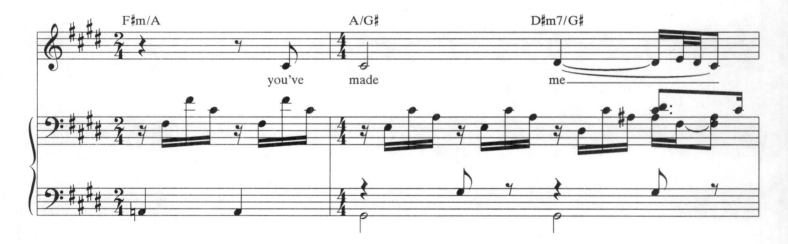

you've   made   me———

whole.

WITHOUT YOU
(From "RENT")

Words and Music by
JONATHAN LARSON

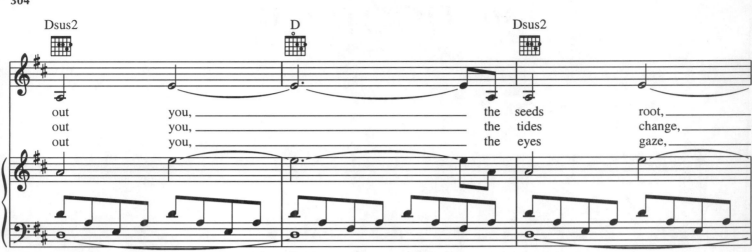

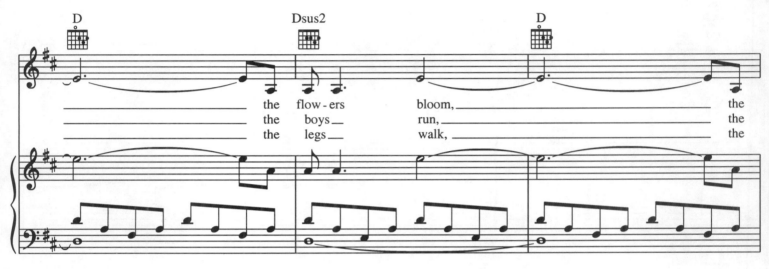

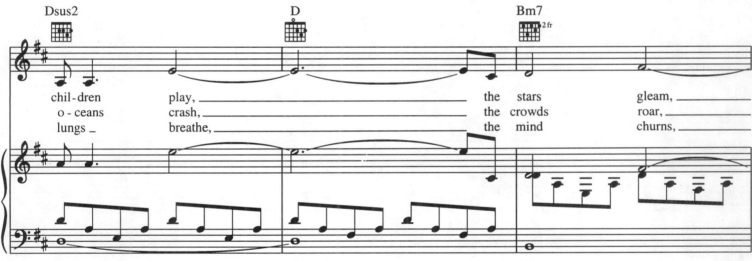

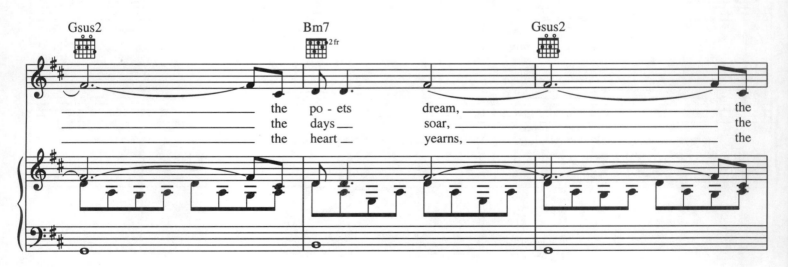

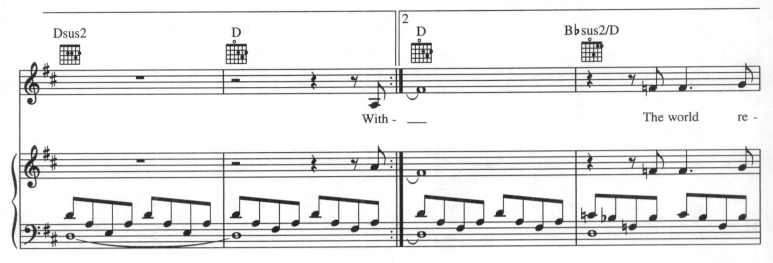

With - __ The world re -

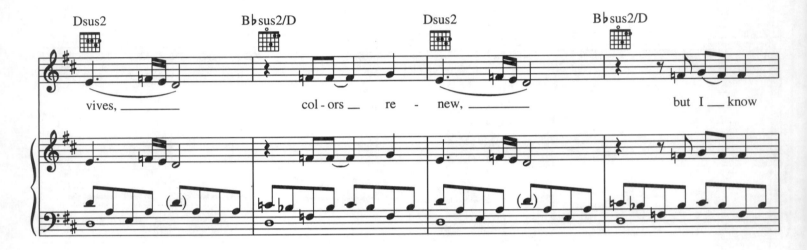

vives, _____ col - ors __ re - new, _____ but I __ know

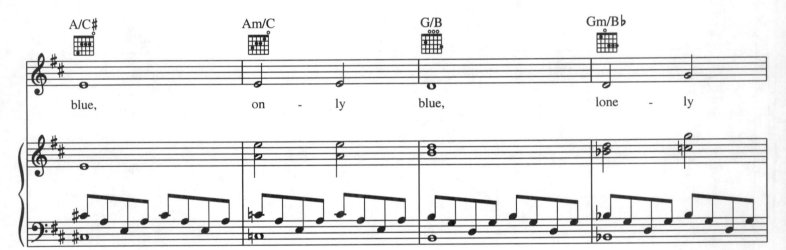

blue, on - ly blue, lone - ly

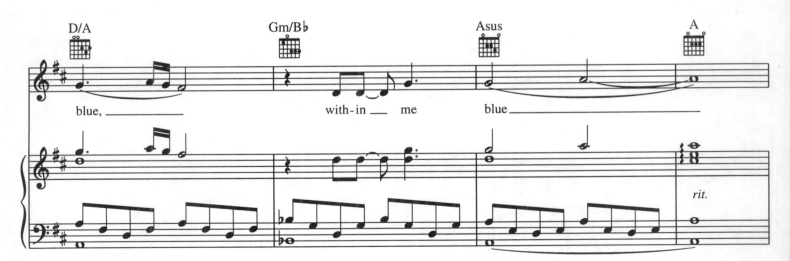

blue, _____ with - in __ me blue _____

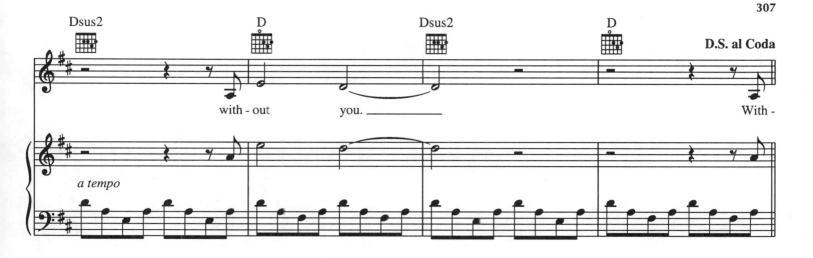

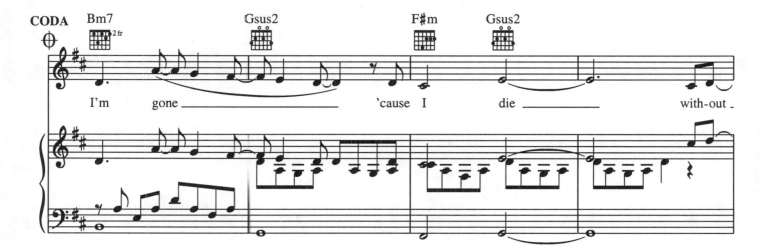

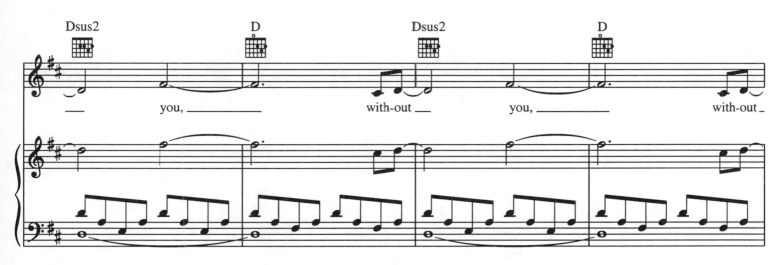

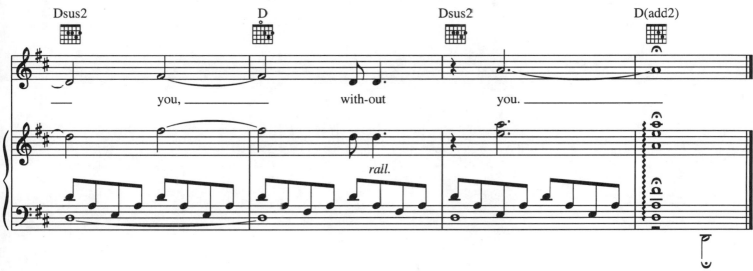

WHO WILL LOVE ME AS I AM?

(From "SIDE SHOW")

Words by BILL RUSSELL
Music by HENRY KRIEGER

310

312

WITH A SONG IN MY HEART

(From "SPRING IS HERE")

Words by LORENZ HART
Music by RICHARD RODGERS

Stacy: Though I know that we meet ev-'ry night And we
Betty: Oh, the moon's not a moon for a night; And these

could-n't have changed since the last time, To my joy and de-light it's a
stars will not twin-kle and fade out! And the words in my ears will re-

new kind of love at first sight. Though it's you and it's I all the
sound for the rest of my years. In the morn-ing I'll find with de-

WITH ONE LOOK

(From "SUNSET BOULEVARD")

Music by ANDREW LLOYD WEBBER
Lyrics by DON BLACK and CHRISTOPHER HAMPTON,
with contributions by AMY POWERS

Lento moderato

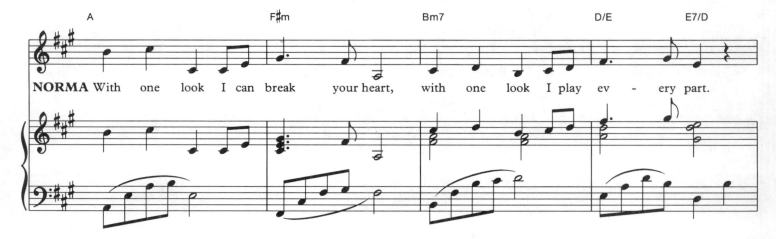

NORMA With one look I can break your heart, with one look I play ev - ery part.

I can make your sad heart sing, with one look you'll know all you need to know.

With one smile I'm the girl next door or the love that you've hun - gered for.

Si - lent mu-sic starts to play, one tear in my eye makes the whole world cry.

With one look they'll for - give the past, they'll re - joice I've re-turned at last

to my peo-ple in the dark, still out there in the dark.

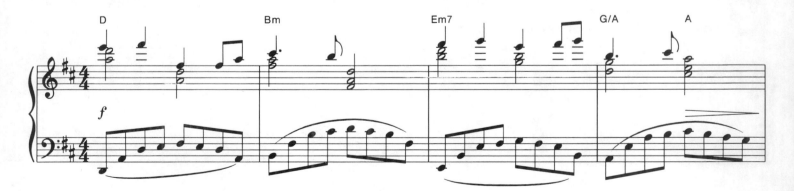

Si - lent mu-sic starts to play. With one look you'll know all you need to know.

With one look I'll ig - nite a blaze, I'll re - turn to my glo - ry days.

They'll say Nor-ma's back at last. This time I am stay-ing, I'm stay-ing for good, I'll be

back where I was born to be, with one look I'll be__ me._____

YOU DON'T KNOW THIS MAN
(From "PARADE")

Music and Lyrics by
JASON ROBERT BROWN

Poco rubato throughout ($\quarternote = 116$)

You don't know this man. You don't know a thing.

You come here with these hor-ri-fy-ing sto-ries, these con-temp-ti-ble con-ceits, and you

say you un-der-stand how a man's heart beats. And you don't know a thing.

You don't know this man.

You don't e - ven try. When a man writes his

moth - er ev - 'ry Sun-day, pays his bills be - fore they're due, works so hard to feed his fam - 'ly, there's your

mur - der - er for you! And you stand here spit - ting words that you know aren't true. Then

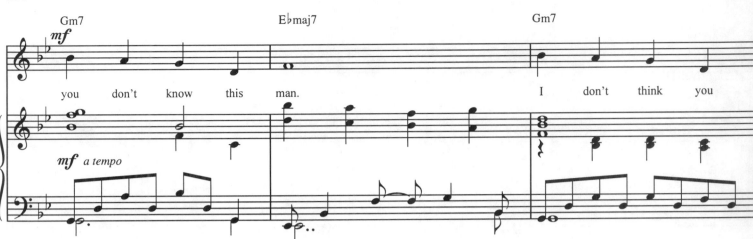
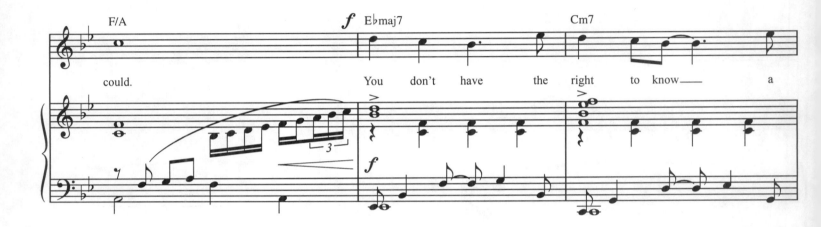

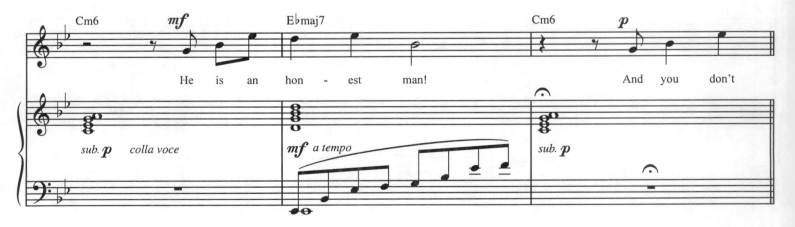

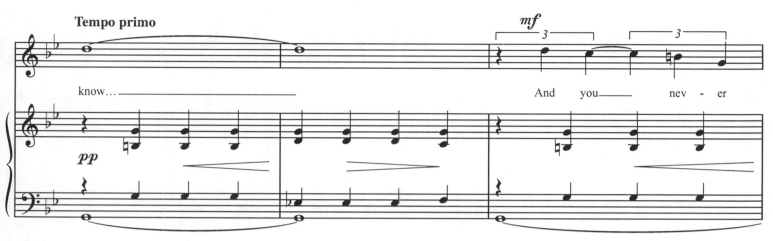

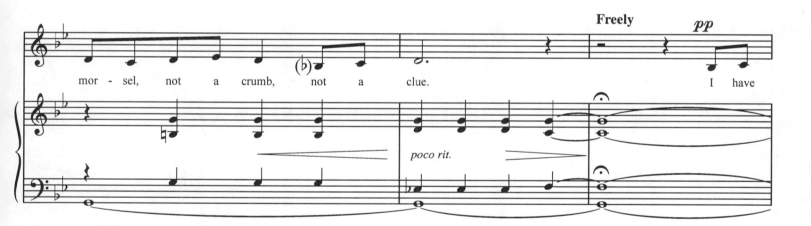

(I WONDER WHY?)
YOU'RE JUST IN LOVE
(From The Stage Production "CALL ME MADAM")

Words and Music by
IRVING BERLIN

I hear sing-ing and there's no one there._

I smell blos-soms and the trees are bare._

All day long I seem to walk on air,_ I won-der

YOU ARE BEAUTIFUL
(From "FLOWER DRUM SONG")

Lyrics by OSCAR HAMMERSTEIN II
Music by RICHARD RODGERS

Refrain *(tranquillo)*